Version: 051719
Page Count: 192
ISBN's:
    9781944607463 (Print Book & PDF)
    9781944607470 (eBook)

Notice: Although IconLogic makes every effort to ensure the accuracy and quality of these materials, all material is provided without any warranty.

Copyright: 2019 by IconLogic, Inc. This document, or any part thereof, may not be reproduced or transmitted in any form or by any means, electronic or mechanical, including photocopying, recording, storage in an information retrieval system, or otherwise, without the prior written permission of IconLogic.

Trademarks: IconLogic, Inc., and the IconLogic logo are registered trademarks of IconLogic. All companies and product names are trademarks or registered trademarks of their respective companies. They are used in this book in an editorial fashion only. No use of any trade name is intended to convey endorsement or other affiliation with IconLogic books.

TechSmith Camtasia 2019
The Essentials

"Skills and Drills" Learning

Kevin Siegel

iCONLOGiC

"Skills and Drills" Learning

Contents

iCONLOGiC

"Skills and Drills" Learning

About This Book

This Section Contains Information About:

The Author

Kevin Siegel is the founder and president of IconLogic, Inc. He has written hundreds of step-by-step computer training books on applications such as *Adobe Captivate, Articulate Storyline, Adobe RoboHelp, Adobe Presenter,* and *TechSmith Camtasia.*

Kevin spent five years in the U.S. Coast Guard as an award-winning photojournalist and has three decades' experience as a trainer, publisher, technical writer, and eLearning developer.

Kevin is a Certified Master Trainer (CMT), Certified Technical Trainer (CTT+), Certified Online Professional Trainer (COTP), and a frequent speaker at trade shows and conventions.

You can reach Kevin at **ksiegel@iconlogic.com**.

IconLogic's Services

Founded in 1992, IconLogic is a training, eLearning development, and publishing company offering services to clients across the globe. As a training company, IconLogic has directly trained thousands of professionals both on-site and online on dozens of applications. As a publishing company, IconLogic has published hundreds of critically acclaimed books and created technical documents for both print and digital publication. And as a development company, IconLogic has produced content for some of the largest companies in the world, including Sanofi Pasteur, Kelsey Seybold, FAA, Office Pro, Duke Energy, Adventist Health System, AGA, PSA Air, AAA, Wells Fargo, American Express, Lockheed Martin, General Mills, Hagerty Insurance, Grange Insurance, Fannie Mae, ADP, ADT, World Bank, Heineken, EverFi, Bank of America, Fresenius Kabi, Wells Fargo, Federal Express, Fannie Mae, American Express, Microsoft, Department of For-Hire Vehicles, Federal Reserve Bank of Richmond, Walmart, USCG, USMC, Canadian Blood, Department of Homeland Security, Canadian Natural Resources, DC Child and Family Services, and the Department of Defense. You can learn more about IconLogic's varied services at www.iconlogic.com.

Book Conventions

Learners learn best by doing, not just by watching or listening. With that simple concept in mind, IconLogic books are created by trainers and/or authors with years of experience training adult learners. Each IconLogic book contains a minimal amount of text and is loaded with hands-on activities, screen captures, and challenge exercises to reinforce newly acquired skills.

This book has been divided into several modules. Because each module builds on lessons learned in a previous module, it is recommended that you complete each module in succession.

Here is the lesson key:

    ❑ instructions for you to follow look like this

If you are expected to type anything or if something is important, it is set in bold type like this:

    ❑ type **9** into the text area

If you are expected to press a key on your keyboard, the instruction looks like this:

    ❑ press [**shift**]

If you have any comments or questions about this book or any IconLogic services, please see the last page of this section for IconLogic's contact information.

Confidence Checks

As you move through the lessons in this book, you will come across the character at the right which indicates a **Confidence Check**. Throughout each module, you are guided through hands-on, step-by-step exercises. But at some point you'll have to fend for yourself. That is where Confidence Checks (also known as challenges) come in. Please be sure to complete each of the challenges because some exercises build on completed Confidence Checks.

Software & Asset Requirements

To complete the lessons presented in this book, you will need TechSmith Camtasia **version 2019** for the Mac or PC installed on your computer. **Camtasia does not come with this book** but a free trial version can be downloaded from TechSmith.com.

You will need to download project assets (data files) that have been created specifically to support this book and this version of Camtasia (See the "Project Files" section below).

You'll be hearing audio throughout the lessons so you'll either need a headset or speakers. And you'll be recording your own voiceover audio so you'll need some sort of microphone.

You will learn how to incorporate Microsoft PowerPoint presentations into Camtasia projects during this book. To complete those activities, you will need a recent version of PowerPoint.

Project Files (Data Files)

During the activities that appear in this book, pretend that you work for a fictional company called Super Simplistic Solutions. As the lead eLearning developer, you must create all of the eLearning content for the company's products, services, and internal processes. During the lessons presented in this book, you will be using Camtasia to create eLearning that might be accessed by learners on all manner of device such as desktop computers, laptops, and mobile devices (such as a phone or tablet). Your mission as you work through this book is to learn Camtasia to create eLearning... it's not necessary for you at this point to come up with the eLearning assets needed to create eLearning (such as videos, images, and audio files). That's where the data files come in. The data files (Camtasia project, audio files, images, videos, etc.) support the lessons presented in this book and can be downloaded from the IconLogic website for free. The process for downloading the Camtasia project assets is below.

Student Activity: Download the Book Project Assets (Data Files)

1. Download the student data files necessary to complete the lessons presented in this book.

   ❑ start a web browser and go to the following web address: **http://www.iconlogic.com**

   ❑ from the top right of the page, click the **Data Files** link

   > Special Pricing   Data Files   Calendar

   ❑ click either **PC** or **Macintosh** (depending on your platform)

   ❑ from the **TechSmith Camtasia Data Files** area, click the **Camtasia 2019: The Essentials** link

NOTES

A dialog box may open, asking if you want to **Save** or **Open** (or **Run**) the file. On some computers and some browsers, the file simply downloads to your Downloads folder without question.

❑ if you receive a **Security message**, click the **Run** button

❑ click the **Save** button and save the file to your computer.

> **PC users**, you are downloading an **exe** file;
> **Mac users**, you are downloading a zipped file

> **PC Users:** The exe files are **not going to install a program on your computer** nor modify your computer in any way (beyond adding some harmless Camtasia projects, videos, images, and audio files to your computer). If you are unable to download the exe version of the files, download the zip version instead using the appropriate link.

❑ after the file downloads, close your browser and locate the file that you just downloaded to your computer.

2. Extract the data files.

❑ **Mac users**, while the zipped file you just downloaded usually extracts automatically, you can manually extract the file by double-clicking it (you can leave the unzipped Camtasia2019Data folder where it is, but it is recommended that you move the unzipped folder to your desktop and work from there)

> **PC users**, double-click the Camtasia2019Data.exe file that you downloaded to open the WinZip Self-Extractor (if prompted, click **Run** and/or **OK** to bypass Windows Defender or other blockers as necessary); then click the **Unzip** button

> **Note:** The default unzip location of the PC assets is **C:**. If you are not permitted to extract files to your C drive, click the **Browse** button and Unzip the files to a location that works best for you.) You can then close the WinZip Self-Extractor.

The data files shown in the image below should now be ready to use on your computer (within in a folder called **Camtasia2019Data**). As you move through the lessons in this book, you will be opening some of them with Camtasia directly and importing other assets (such as audio files) into Camtasia. When you have completed the lessons in this book, you can delete both the Camtasia2019Data folder and the zipped file you downloaded to your computer.

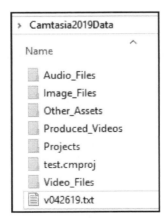

How Software Updates Affect This Book

This book was written specifically to teach you how to use TechSmith Camtasia **version 2019**. At the time this book was written, Camtasia 2019 was the latest and greatest version of Camtasia available from TechSmith.

With each major release of Camtasia, my intention is to write a new book to support that version and make it available within 30-60 days of the software being released by TechSmith. From time to time, TechSmith makes service releases/patches of Camtasia available for customers that fix bugs or add functionality. For instance, I would expect TechSmith to update Camtasia with a patch or two within a few months of Camtasia 2019 being released. That patched version might be called Camtasia **2019.0.1** or perhaps **2019.1**. You can check your Camtasia version by choosing **Help > About Camtasia** if you're on a PC (first image below); **Camtasia 2019 > About Camtasia** if you're on a Mac (second image below).

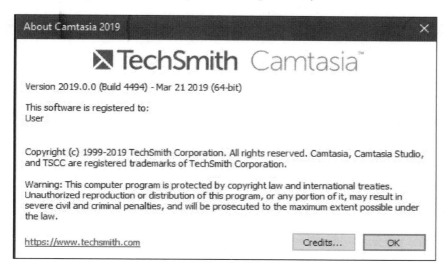

Usually these updates are minor (bug fixes) and have little or no impact on the lessons presented in this book. However, TechSmith sometimes makes significant changes to the way Camtasia looks or behaves, even with minor patches. (Such was the case when TechSmith updated Camtasia from version 8.3 to 8.4—several features were changed throwing readers of my books into a tizzy.)

Because it is not possible for me to recall and update printed books, some instructions you are asked to follow in this book may not match the patched/updated version of Camtasia that you

might be using. If something on your screen does not match what is showing in the book, please visit the Errata page on the IconLogic website (http://www.iconlogic.com/skills-drills-workbooks/errata-pages-return-policy.html or contact me directly at ksiegel@iconlogic.com).

Contacting IconLogic

Web: **www.iconlogic.com**

Phone: **888.812.4827**

Email: **info@iconlogic.com**

iCONLOGiC

"Skills and Drills" Learning

Rank Your Skills

Before starting this book, complete the skills assessment on the next page.

Skills Assessment

How this assessment works

Below you will find 10 course objectives for *TechSmith Camtasia 2019: The Essentials*. **Before starting the book:** Review each objective and rank your skills using the scale next to each objective. A rank of ① means **No Confidence** in the skill. A rank of ⑤ means **Total Confidence**. After you've completed this assessment, go through the entire book. **After finishing the book:** Review each objective and rank your skills now that you've completed the book. Most people see dramatic improvements in the second assessment after completing the lessons in this book.

Before-Class Skills Assessment

1. I can add media to the Media Bin.   ① ② ③ ④ ⑤
2. I can add a Quiz to a Project.   ① ② ③ ④ ⑤
3. I can create Captions.   ① ② ③ ④ ⑤
4. I can share Camtasia projects on YouTube.   ① ② ③ ④ ⑤
5. I can record voiceover audio within Camtasia.   ① ② ③ ④ ⑤
6. I can add objects to a project from the Library.   ① ② ③ ④ ⑤
7. I can create an animation with Behaviors.   ① ② ③ ④ ⑤
8. I can edit an audio file within Camtasia.   ① ② ③ ④ ⑤
9. I can upload content to Screencast.com.   ① ② ③ ④ ⑤
10. I can record screen actions using the Recorder.   ① ② ③ ④ ⑤

After-Class Skills Assessment

1. I can add media to the Media Bin.   ① ② ③ ④ ⑤
2. I can add a Quiz to a Project.   ① ② ③ ④ ⑤
3. I can create Captions.   ① ② ③ ④ ⑤
4. I can share Camtasia projects on YouTube.   ① ② ③ ④ ⑤
5. I can record voiceover audio within Camtasia.   ① ② ③ ④ ⑤
6. I can add objects to a project from the Library.   ① ② ③ ④ ⑤
7. I can create an animation with Behaviors.   ① ② ③ ④ ⑤
8. I can edit an audio file within Camtasia.   ① ② ③ ④ ⑤
9. I can upload content to Screencast.com.   ① ② ③ ④ ⑤
10. I can record screen actions using the Recorder.   ① ② ③ ④ ⑤

iCONLOGiC
"Skills and Drills" Learning

Preface

In This Module You Will Learn About:

Education Through Pictures

In a previous life, I was a professional photographer. When I wasn't snapping photos during a five-year tour with the U.S. Coast Guard, I covered media events in New York City as a freelance photographer.

Just about any photographer will tell you that the goal when taking pictures is to capture a story with a few, or maybe just one, photograph. I'm betting that you have heard the saying "a picture is worth a thousand words" more than once. As a professional photographer, I lived those words.

I have spent the bulk of my career attempting to perfect the art of teaching complex concepts to busy, distracted adult learners. I have always attempted to write documentation using as few words as possible and to teach lessons as efficiently as possible.

If you are in the business of educating, you know how difficult the job of writing relevant lesson plans with fewer and fewer words can be. My step-by-step workbooks have long been known for their "skills-and-drills learning" approach. The term "skills-and-drills" learning means different things to different people. For some, it means fast-moving lessons that do not drown a person with unnecessary information. For me, "skills-and-drills learning" means learning something by doing, whatever that something is. It also means learning with a heavy dose of imagery instead of a heavy dose of text.

I learned long ago that people tend to think not with words but with pictures. Here's an example of what I mean.

> Close your eyes for a second and picture **three** in your mind's eye. Open your eyes after a few seconds and read on. (See how precise I am? I know that some of you would have closed your eyes, kept them closed, and then fallen asleep without the last instruction.)

I wasn't specific when I asked you to picture **three** was I? Because I didn't tell you how to picture *three*, it's a good bet that things such as *three cupcakes, three bowls of ice cream,* or *three big boxes of Cap'n Crunch* (everyone knows that the Cap'n is the best breakfast cereal *ever*) flashed into your mind's eye.

Perhaps a large numeral 3 appeared in your mind's eye—not the word "three." In fact, I doubt that you visualized the word *three*. Why? As I said above, most people think in terms of pictures, not words. That's the reason my books usually contain hundreds of screen captures that visually show concepts that might have taken several paragraphs to explain. And when I do have to explain a concept, I make every effort to minimize the chatter and get right to the point.

Planning eLearning Lessons

By the time you finish this workbook, you will have a better understanding of how to create technically solid eLearning lessons using Camtasia. However, that does not necessarily mean you will create *good* eLearning lessons. If you want to create good, useful lessons, plan ahead by asking yourself the following questions:

☐ **What lessons do I want to make available as eLearning lessons?** If you are creating an eLearning course that is based on a traditional classroom course, not every lesson will be appropriate for eLearning. In addition, keep in mind that eLearning lessons aren't social events, they are completed by students who are working alone. Any lessons intended for groups may need to be removed from the course or modified to work in an online environment.

☐ **Have I written a script(s)?** If you are going to capture a screen process such as the various mouse clicks performed within an application, it is critical that you document the process prior to recording anything using Camtasia Recorder. If you're going to include voiceover audio in your eLearning, you'll need a second script: **a voiceover script** that will be used when you record the voiceover audio yourself (or you can send the script to a voiceover recording specialist who will record your script and send you audio files you'll import into Camtasia).

☐ **Do I want my projects to contain images and sound effects?** Images and sound effects enhance the eLearning experience, but where will you find those assets? The Internet is a wonderful resource, but be careful; assets found on the Internet are rarely free and are often protected by copyright laws.

☐ **Will there be screen text?** Callouts (Annotations) are written instructions and/or descriptions that describe what is occurring onscreen. Adding this text in the Editor is easy, but somebody will have to write and proofread the text at some point. Keep in mind that Camtasia does not include a spell-check feature. If you're going to support learners with hearing disabilities, you'll need to include closed captions. The captions will be added to the Camtasia Timeline and while not difficult to add, take time.

☐ **What is the average reading level of my audience?** Consider your audience and write content that everyone can consume. The lower the reading level of your audience, the longer it will take for learners to read the annotations. In this workbook, you will learn how to set the timing for the callouts. However, you will need to determine the appropriate pace.

☐ **What font, font size, and colors will I use?** Because reading text onscreen is not as easy as reading printed content, carefully consider your font choices. Verdana and Calibri are two popular font choices. A dark font color works well when you use a light background.

When planning projects, keep in mind that the most useful projects contain the following basic elements (you will learn how to add these elements as you move through this workbook):

☐ A Title Scene (telling the audience what they are going to learn)

☐ Credits and Copyright Scene

☐ Narration, Music, and Other Sound Effects (as appropriate)

☐ Images and Animations (as appropriate)

☐ Some Interactivity (such as Hotspots and Quizzes)

☐ An Ending Scene (reviewing what the audience learned)

eLearning Development Phases

The infographic below offers a visual way to think about the eLearning development process and phases. A larger version of the graphic can be downloaded from www.iconlogic.com/skills-drills-workbooks/elearning-resources.html.

eLearning Development Phases

1 **DISCOVERY**
Meet with the client. Find out **what they want** in an ideal eLearning course. Who is the **audience**? Define a course **mission statement** for the course in general. You'll also need a mission statement for each lesson in the course. Will the course require **accessibility**? **Audio**? Will it need to be **localized**? What kind of **hardware** will students be using to access the course?

DESIGN **2**
Which tool will you be using to develop the content (**Camtasia, Captivate**, **Presenter**, **Storyline**, or perhaps a combination of a couple tools)? **Instructional design**, a **graphical treatment**, and **navigational choices** are now made and implemented.

3 **WRITING and/or STORYBOARDING**
Now that you have chosen a production tool and decided the overall design of the course, you'll need to **plot out the flow** of the course and **write a script and/or a storyboard**. If the course includes voiceover audio, you'll need a separate (and different) script for that.

PRODUCTION **4**
Now it's time to get busy with the **development work** in the selected tool. This includes everything right up to the point of publishing. You'll also **beta test** the lessons in this phase as they are completed.

5 **CLIENT APPROVAL**
You're almost there! But, before project completion, you'll need to get your **client's approval**. Depending upon how this goes, **you may need to repeat parts of steps two, three, and four**.

PUBLISHING and IMPLEMENTATION **6**
This includes not only **publishing locally**, but uploading the content to a **web server** or **LMS (SCORM or AICC)**. Be sure to allow time to work out bugs in this phase.

7 **MAINTENANCE**
You did a great job! But sometimes changes and updates are necessary. This phase includes **making updates** to the content and **re-posting to the LMS or web server**.

Brought to you by:

Camtasia Production Times (Level of Effort)

When I say production time, I'm referring to the actual time you will spend editing a Camtasia project. It may sound like common sense, but the longer each video plays, the longer it will typically take for you to produce it in Camtasia. Many new developers underestimate the number of hours needed to produce eLearning. The following table should help.

Project Size	Number of Production Hours
Small Videos (1-3 minutes of play time)	2-6 hours
Medium Videos (4-6 minutes)	8-12 hours
Long Videos (7-10 minutes)	14-20 hours
Extra-Long Videos (more than 10 minutes)	Consider splitting videos this large into smaller Camtasia projects.

Project Size and Display Resolution

Several years ago, monitors were small and display resolutions low. A display resolution of 800 x 600 pixels was common. If you developed eLearning content for a display that small, a Camtasia canvas size of 640 x 480 worked well.

A few years later, 1024 x 768 was the standard display resolution, resulting in typical Camtasia projects sized to 800 x 600.

According to **w3schools.com**, a typical desktop screen resolution today is 1366 x 768, and it's trending higher.

What's the ideal size for a Camtasia project? Unfortunately, there isn't a cookie-cutter answer. The width and height of a software demonstration you record depends largely on the size of your display, your display resolution, and the software you're recording (some software cannot be resized and may need to take up your entire display).

When I record my screen using the Camtasia recorder, I always use the same computer to record all of the project videos for a course.

Video cards and display sizes vary from computer to computer and manufacturer to manufacturer. I want my course recordings to look consistent so I always use the same computer, same resolution, same color theme, and same size Camtasia Recorder recording area.

In the image at the right, notice the suggested Canvas Dimensions (also known as the Project Size) available in Camtasia 2019.

According to TechSmith, if you are creating content for learners on Instagram, consider a Canvas size of 640 x 640. FaceBook video? Think 820 x 462. YouTube? Consider a project size of 1902 x 1080 or 1280 x 720.

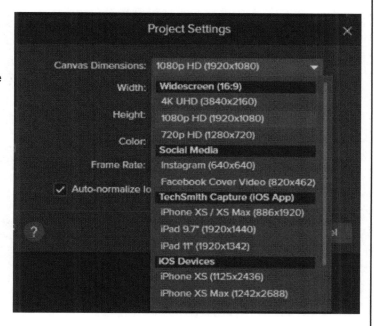

Design Best Practices

Much of what you do in Camtasia will feel similar to what you can do in Microsoft PowerPoint. If you've used PowerPoint you are familiar with adding objects to a slide. In Camtasia, you add objects to the Canvas and use the Timeline to control when those objects are seen by the learner. Unlike PowerPoint, which can contain hundreds of slides, there is only one Canvas in Camtasia, and only one Timeline.

You don't have to be a seasoned designer to produce beautiful and effective Camtasia projects. Here are a few tips to get you started:

- ❑ If you're creating the content in PowerPoint, there are occasions when a bulleted list is the best way to convey an idea. Although PowerPoint uses a bulleted approach to information by default, you do not have to use that format in eLearning.

- ❑ Try splitting the bullets into separate slides with a single image to illustrate each point, or forgo the text and replace it with a chart, diagram, or other informative/interesting image.

- ❑ It is not necessary to have every bit of information you cover on the screen at one time. Encourage your audience to listen and, if necessary, take notes based on what you say, not what is shown on the screen.

- ❑ Few learners are impressed with how many moving, colorful objects each slide contains. When it comes to eLearning, the old saying, "content is King," has never been more appropriate. Ensure each of your screens contain relevant, need-to-know information and that the information is presented as clutter-free as possible.

- ❑ Consider taking more of a photographic approach to the images you use. You can easily find stock photographs on the web using any one of a number of pay-for-use websites. There are many free sites, but keep in mind that to save time and frustration (and improve on the selection and quality), you might want to set aside a budget to pay for images.

Fonts and eLearning

The most important thing about eLearning is solid content. But could you be inadvertently making your content harder to read and understand by using the wrong fonts? Is good font selection really important? Read on to discover the many surprising ways fonts can affect your content.

Some Fonts Read Better On-Screen

eCommerce Consultant Dr. Ralph F. Wilson did a study in 2001 to determine if serif fonts (fonts with little lines on the tops and bottoms of characters, such as Times New Roman) or sans serif fonts (those without lines, such as Arial) were more suited to being read on computer monitors. His study concluded that although Times New Roman is easily read in printed materials, the lower resolution of monitors (72 dots per inch (dpi) versus 180 dpi or higher) makes it much more difficult to read in digital format. Times New Roman 12 pt was pitted against Arial 12 pt with respondents finding the sans serif Arial font more readable at a rate of two to one.

Lorem ipsum frangali puttuto rigali fortuitous confulence magficati alorem. Lorem ipsum frangali puttuto rigali fortuitous confulence magficati alorem.	Lorem ipsum frangali puttuto rigali fortuitous confulence magficati alorem. Lorem ipsum frangali puttuto rigali fortuitous confulence magficati alorem.
Times New Roman 12 pt	Arial 12 pt
520	1123
32%	68%

Source: http://www.practicalecommerce.com/articles/100159-html-email-fonts

Wilson also tested the readability of Arial versus Verdana on computer screens and found that in font sizes greater than 10 pt, Arial was more readable, whereas Verdana was more readable in font sizes 10 pt and smaller.

So should you stop using Times New Roman in your eLearning lessons? Not completely. For instance, you can use Times New Roman for text content that is not expected to be read quickly.

Some Fonts Increase Trust

A 2008 study by Sharath Sasidharan and Ganga Dhanesh for the Association of Information Systems found that typography can affect trust in eCommerce. The study found that to instill trust in online consumers, you should keep it simple: "To the extent possible, particularly for websites that need to engage in financial transactions or collect personal information from their users, the dominant typeface used to present text material should be a serif or sans serif font such as Times New Roman or Arial."

If you feel your eLearning content will be presented to a skeptical audience (or one you've never worked with before), dazzling them with fancy fonts may not be the way to go. You can use fancy fonts from time to time to break up the monotony of a dry lesson, but consider using such nonstandard fonts sparingly. Use the fancy fonts for headings or as accents but not for the bulk of your text.

The Readability of Fonts Affects Participation

A study done at the University of Michigan in 2008 on typecase in instructions found that the ease with which a font in instructional material is read can have an impact on the perceived skill level needed to complete a task.

The study found that if directions are presented in a font that is deemed more difficult to read, "the task will be viewed as being difficult, taking a long time to complete and perhaps, not even worth trying."

The results of the study by Wilson indicate that it is probably not a good idea to present eLearning material, especially to beginners, in a Times New Roman font, as it may make the information seem too difficult to process or overwhelming.

Popular eLearning Fonts

I polled my "Skills & Drills" newsletter readers and asked which fonts they tended to use in eLearning. Here is a list of the most popular fonts:

- ☐ Verdana
- ☐ Helvetica
- ☐ Arial
- ☐ Calibri
- ☐ Times
- ☐ Palatino
- ☐ Times New Roman
- ☐ Century Schoolbook (for print)

Fonts and Personas

If you are creating eLearning for business professionals, you might want to use a different font in your design than you would if you were creating eLearning for high school students. But what font would you use if you want to convey a feeling of happiness? Formality? Cuddliness?

In a study (funded by Microsoft) by A. Dawn Shaikh, Barbara S. Chaparro, and Doug Fox, the perceived personality traits of fonts were categorized. The table below shows the top three fonts for each personality objective.

	Top Three		
Stable	TNR	Arial	Cambria
Flexible	Kristen	Gigi	Rage Italic
Conformist	Courier New	TNR	Arial
Polite	Monotype Corsiva	TNR	Cambria
Mature	TNR	Courier New	Cambria
Formal	TNR	Monotype Corsiva	Georgia
Assertive	**Impact**	**Rockwell Xbold**	Georgia
Practical	Georgia	TNR	Cambria
Creative	Gigi	Kristen	Rage Italic
Happy	Kristen	Gigi	Comic Sans
Exciting	Gigi	Kristen	Rage Italic
Attractive	Monotype Corsiva	Rage Italic	Gigi
Elegant	Monotype Corsiva	Rage Italic	Gigi
Cuddly	Kristen	Gigi	Comic Sans
Feminine	Gigi	Monotype Corsiva	Kristen
Unstable	Gigi	Kristen	Rage Italic
Rigid	**Impact**	Courier New	Agency FB
Rebel	Gigi	Kristen	Rage Italic
Rude	**Impact**	**Rockwell Xbold**	Agency FB
Youthful	Kristen	Gigi	Comic Sans
Casual	Kristen	Comic Sans	Gigi
Passive	Kristen	Gigi	Comic Sans
Impractical	Gigi	Rage Italic	Kristen
Unimaginative	Courier New	Arial	Consolas
Sad	**Impact**	Courier New	Agency FB
Dull	Courier New	Consolas	Verdana
Unattractive	**Impact**	Courier New	**Rockwell Xbold**
Plain	Courier New	**Impact**	**Rockwell Xbold**
Coarse	**Impact**	**Rockwell Xbold**	Courier New
Masculine	**Impact**	**Rockwell Xbold**	Courier New

Source: http://usabilitynews.org/perception-of-fonts-perceived-personality-traits-and-uses/

Notes

iCONLOGiC

"Skills and Drills" Learning

Module 1: Exploring Camtasia

In This Module You Will Learn About

And You Will Learn To

The Camtasia Interface

As you work through the lessons in this book, my goal is to get you comfortable with each specific Camtasia area or feature before proceeding. Like any feature-rich program, mastering Camtasia is going to be a marathon, not a sprint. Soon enough you'll be in full stride, creating awesome eLearning content using Camtasia. But before the sprint to the finish line comes the marathon itself. During these first few activities, I'd like to give you a chance to familiarize yourself with Camtasia's workspace. Specifically, you'll start Camtasia, become familiar with the Getting Started project, open an existing project, and poke around Camtasia's interface a bit.

Student Activity: Open a Camtasia Project

1. Start Camtasia 2019.

   If this is your first time starting Camtasia, a **Getting Started** project has likely opened by itself, and it's playing. To stop the sample project from playing, look to the right side of the screen and you'll see a playbar centered just beneath the preview. Click the **Pause** button on the playbar (shown in the second image below) to stop the preview.

   The playback controls shown above left are from Camtasia for Windows. Above right is Camtasia for Mac. Notice the subtle differences between the two platforms (the controls on the Windows side include keyboard shortcuts for playback; the Mac side does not display the shortcuts. When the differences between the two platforms are subtle, as shown above, I'll rarely mention them again. When the differences are significant, I'll call them out with platform-specific steps and/or screen shots.

   If this isn't your first time starting Camtasia or you have already created a project or two, I'm betting that the Getting Started project did not open at all. If you're curious to see the Getting Started project, you can open it at any time by choosing **Help > Open Getting Started Project**. (If the **Help** menu isn't available, you'll first need to create a New Project by clicking **New Project** on the Welcome window.)

The picture below is an example of what you will typically see the second time you start Camtasia. By default, there is a **Welcome** window on the screen.

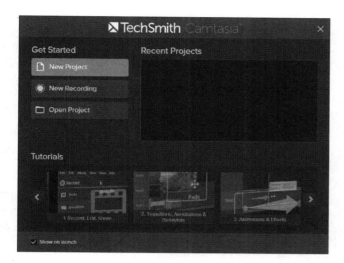

At this point, it does not matter if a project is open. The important thing is to ensure you have started Camtasia. Also, if you have not yet downloaded the IconLogic project assets (also known as Data Files), turn to the **About This Book** section at the beginning of this book and work through the **Download the Book Project Assets (Data Files)** activity on page vii.

2. Open a project from the Camtasia2019Data, Projects folder.

   ☐ if the **Welcome** window (shown above) is on your screen, click the **Open Project** button; if a Camtasia project is currently open, choose **File > Open Project**

   The **Open** dialog box appears.

   ☐ navigate to **Camtasia2019Data** folder on your computer

   ☐ open the **Projects** folder

   ☐ open **Demo**

   The entire screen that you see (from the **File** menu in the upper left to the objects along the bottom of the window) is known as the **Editor**. There are several things to explore within the Editor, which you will do soon enough. First, let's see what happens if you decide to create a new project.

3. Create a new project.

   ☐ choose **File > New Project** (if prompted, don't save the Demo project)

   You are probably used to programs that allow you to open multiple projects concurrently and switch between them. On the Mac version of Camtasia, you can switch between open projects via the Window menu. On the PC, you can have only one Camtasia project open at any one time so the Demo project closes when the new project is created.

4. Open a recent project.

   ☐ choose **File > Recent Projects > Demo**

   The Demo project should once again be open, ready for you to explore.

Student Activity: Explore Camtasia's Tools

1. Ensure that the **Demo** project is open.

2. View the Voice Narration panel.

    ☐ choose **View > Tools > Voice Narration**

   The Voice Narration panel appears in the upper left of the Editor. The panel is used to record your voice (assuming you have a microphone attached to your computer). You will learn to record voiceover audio beginning on page 92.

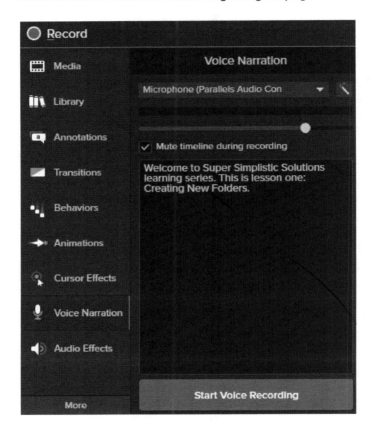

   Note: You can access the Voice Narration options via the list of tools at the left. Depending upon the size of your screen, you may not see all of the tools shown in the image above. In that case, you can access the missing tools by clicking **More**.

3. Show the Annotations panel.

    ☐ from the list of tools at the left, click **Annotations**

   There are six types of Annotations that allow you to help grab the learner's attention (including Callouts, Arrows and Lines, Shapes, Sketch, and Keystroke images). You will learn to add Annotations beginning on page 70.

4. Show the Transitions panel.

❑ from the list of tools at the left, click **Transitions**

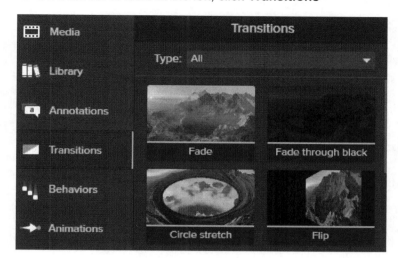

Transitions give you the ability to move from one part of your lesson to another using professional animation effects. You'll learn how to add Transitions to a project beginning on page 82.

Next you will explore the Media Bin and the Library.

The Media Bin and Library

Every new Camtasia project has a Media Bin... but it's empty. You import assets, such as images, into the Media Bin as needed. Once assets are imported into the Media Bin, you can add them to the Camtasia Timeline. Each project contains its own unique Media Bin. Unfortunately, you cannot share Media Bins across projects. By contrast, the Library comes preloaded with assets provided by TechSmith including animations, icons, and music. Library assets are available to use in any project right away. All you need to do is select the asset(s) and add it to the Timeline.

Student Activity: Explore the Media Bin and Library

1. Ensure that the **Demo** project is open.

2. View the Media Bin.

    ☐ from the list of tools at the left, click **Media**

    There are a several assets in this project's Media Bin including videos, images, and audio.

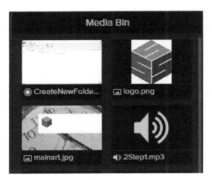

The default view for the Media Bin is Thumbnails, which is nice if you want a decent-sized preview of the Media Bin assets. However, many developers prefer the organized look and feel of the Details view.

3. Change the Media Bin view from Thumbnails to Details.

    ☐ at the bottom right of the **Media Bin,** click the **Details** icon

Type	Name	Duration
◉	CreateNewFolderVideo.tre	0:00:18;15
🖼	logo.png	
🖼	mainart.jpg	
🔊	2Step1.mp3	0:01:04
🔊	audio_file01.wav	0:00:06
🔊	audio_file03.wav	0:00:23
🔊	audio_file04.wav	0:00:18
🔊	audio_file02.wav	0:00:08
🔊	audio_file05.wav	0:00:17
◉	RenameFolderVideo.trec	0:00:17;09
🔊	audio_file06.wav	0:00:27
🔊	audio_file07.wav	0:00:26
◉	DeleteFolder.trec	0:00:08;04
◉	RestoreFolder.trec	0:00:24;12

4. Change the Media Bin view from Details back to Thumbnails.

   ❏ at the bottom right of the Media Bin, click the **Thumbnails** icon

   You will learn how to add assets to the Media Bin beginning on page 52.

5. Show the Library panel.

   ❏ from the list of tools at the left, click **Library**

   The Library takes the place of the Media Bin. By default, there are several folders within the Library containing myriad images, animations, and audio files. You can create your own folders and import your own assets into the Library. Also, there is a link at the bottom of the Library labeled "Download more assets." For $199 per year, TechSmith provides access to hundreds of thousands of videos, images, and audio files you can use in your Camtasia project. You won't need the subscription to complete this book (you'll be using the free assets currently in the Library) but should you be unable to find specific assets, the subscription might be a viable option for you down the road.

   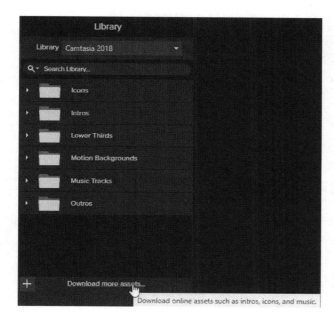

6. Explore a Library folder.

   ❏ from the Library, click the triangle to the left of **Music Tracks**

   The folder opens and displays several assets.

   It is simple to add any of these assets to your project—a drag and drop is all it takes. You will get a chance to do that later. For now, let's continue the Camtasia tour.

7. Preview a Library asset.

☐ on the **Library**, double-click any music asset

A preview window opens and, assuming you have speakers or a headset, you will hear the music. (You can preview images and video is the same manner.)

☐ close the Preview window

You will learn how to add music from the Library to a project later.

The Canvas and Timeline

The Canvas, which is at the right of the Editor, offers an excellent way to position screen elements and preview the project as you're working. As you preview a project via the Canvas, you'll be able to use the Timeline to keep track of what's happening in your project and when.

The Timeline is at the bottom of the Editor. As its name implies, the Timeline is used to control the timing of objects added to the Canvas. For instance, using the Timeline, you can force objects such as images or videos to appear at the same time, or you can force one object to appear as another goes away. You'll learn to use both the Canvas and Timeline as you move through lessons in this book. For now, you'll use the Canvas to preview the assets added to the Timeline of the demo project.

Student Activity: Preview a Project

1. Ensure that the **Demo** project is open.

2. Preview the project.

   ☐ on the **Canvas**, click **Play** tool

   As the lesson plays on the Canvas, notice that a thin line and strange-looking object moves across the Timeline. The object is known as the Playhead (it has both a green and a red square, which you will learn about later). The Playhead and thin line show you where the preview is in relation to the Timeline. You will learn to work with the Timeline as you progress through the lessons in this book.

   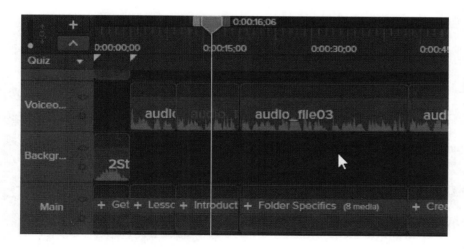

3. Detach the Canvas.

   ☐ choose **View > Canvas > Detach Canvas** (you can also find this option in the **Canvas Options** drop-down menu located just above the Canvas)

   Click the menu located just above the **Preview** area (the Preview is also known as the **Canvas**) the find the **Detach Canvas** menu item.

The Canvas detaches from Editor. You can now position the panel anywhere on your display that you like.

4. Explore Full Screen Mode.

   ❏ with the Canvas detached, click the **Full Screen** button (in the lower right of the Canvas)

   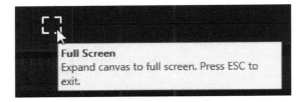

   While in Full Screen mode, you can see the lesson but not the Camtasia interface.

5. Exit Full Screen mode.

   ❏ press [**esc**] on your keyboard

6. Attach the Canvas.

   ❏ from the top of the detached Canvas, click the **Canvas Options** drop-down menu (shown below) and choose **Attach Canvas**

   The Canvas reattaches to the upper right of the Editor.

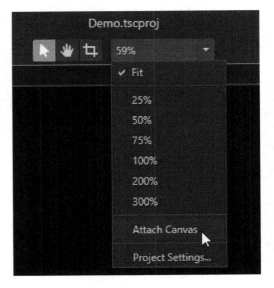

7. Use a keyboard shortcut to Zoom closer and farther away from the Canvas.

   ❑ PC users, press [**ctrl**] [**=**]; Mac users press [**command**] [**=**] a few times to zoom closer to the Canvas

   ❑ PC users, press [**ctrl**] [**+**]; Mac users press [**command**] [**+**] a few times to zoom away from the Canvas

8. Modify the Canvas zooming keyboard shortcuts.

   ❑ PC users, choose **Edit > Preferences**; Mac users, choose **Camtasia 2019 > Preferences**

   The Preferences dialog box opens.

   ❑ select the **Shortcuts** tab

   ❑ select **Canvas Options**

   ❑ to the right of Zoom in on Canvas, click the current keyboard shortcut and replace it with [**ctrl**] [**shift**] [**=**] on the PC and [**command**] [**shift**] [**=**] on the Mac

Zoom in on canvas	Ctrl+Shift+=
Zoom out on canvas	Ctrl+-
Enable/disable canvas snapping	Ctrl+;

Restore Defaults	
Zoom in on canvas:	⇧⌘=
Zoom out on canvas:	⌘-

   ❑ PC users, click the **OK** button; Mac users, close the Shortcuts dialog box

9. Test the modified keyboard shortcuts.

   ❑ PC users, press [**ctrl**] [**shift**] [**=**]; Mac users press [**command**] [**shift**] [**=**] a few times to zoom closer to the Canvas

   ❑ PC users, press [**ctrl**] [**+**]; Mac users press [**command**] [**+**] a few times to zoom away from the Canvas

10. Restore the keyboard shortcuts to their defaults.

   ❑ PC users, choose **Edit > Preferences**; Mac users, choose **Camtasia 2019 > Preferences**

   The Preferences dialog box reopens.

   ❑ select the **Shortcuts** tab

   ❑ click the **Restore Defaults** button

   ❑ PC users, click the **OK** button; Mac users, close the Shortcuts dialog box

   As you continue to learn Camtasia, keep in mind that there are dozens of keyboard shortcuts for adding animations, captions, quizzes, markers and more,. You should spend

↑NOTES↑

some time exploring more of the available shortcuts and customize them to suit your needs.

11. Quit Camtasia (PC users: **File > Exit**; Mac users: **File > Quit**).

There is no need to save any changes made to the Demo project (if prompted).

iCONLOGiC

"Skills and Drills" Learning

Module 2: Recording Videos

In This Module You Will Learn About:

And You Will Learn To:

Rehearsals

You have been hired to create an eLearning course that teaches new employees at your company how to use **Notepad** (PC) or **TextEdit** (Mac). One of the lessons you plan to record using Camtasia includes how to change the page orientation within Notepad.

Here is a sample script showing the kind of detailed, step-by-step instructions you need to create or receive from a Subject Matter Expert (SME). You are expected to perform each step written below in Notepad or TextEdit.

Dear Camtasia developer, while using Notepad or TextEdit, record the process of changing the Page Orientation from Portrait to Landscape and then back again (from Landscape to Portrait). Create the video using a computer display resolution and screen capture size that you think is best. Thanks. Your pal, the Subject Matter Expert.

1. From within Notepad or TextEdit, click the **File** menu.

2. Click the **Page Setup** menu item.

3. Click the **Landscape** orientation button.

4. Click the **OK** button.

5. Click the **File** menu.

6. Click the **Page Setup** menu item.

7. Click the **Portrait** orientation button.

8. Click the **OK** button.

9. Stop the recording process (you're done).

The script sounds simple. However, you will not know what kind of trouble you are going to get into unless you rehearse the script prior to recording the process with Camtasia. Let's run a rehearsal, just as if you were a big-time movie director and you were in charge of a blockbuster movie.

Places everyone, and quiet on the set.

Student Activity: Rehearse a Script

1. Start Notepad or TextEdit.

   The process of starting either Notepad or TextEdit varies slightly, depending on your operating system. For instance, if you are using Windows 7, choose **Start**, type **notepad**, and press [**enter**]. If you are using Windows 8 or newer, use the **Search** feature to start Notepad. If you are using a Mac, choose **Go > Applications**. Locate and then open **TextEdit**, and then create a New document.

   In the images below, Notepad is pictured at the left; TextEdit is at the right.

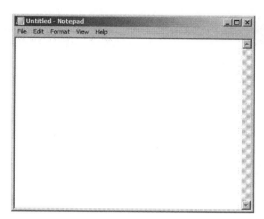 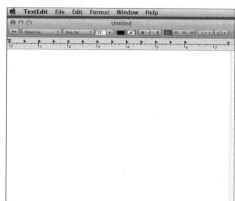

2. Rehearse the script.

   ☐ using **Notepad** for **TextEdit** (not Camtasia), click the **File** menu

   ☐ click the **Page Setup** menu item

   ☐ from the **Orientation** area, click **Landscape**

   ☐ click the **OK** button

   ☐ click the **File** menu

   ☐ click the **Page Setup** menu item

   ☐ click the **Portrait** orientation button

   ☐ click the **OK** button

   Hey, look at that! The script worked perfectly... no surprises. You are now ready to work the exact steps again. Only this time, you will record every click that you make. During the recording process, Camtasia creates a video of the entire process.

Recording Screen Actions

When you record screen actions using Camtasia, you should pretend you are using a video recorder and creating a movie (you're both the director and the producer). During the recording process, everything you do is recorded exactly as you do it. Every delay, every good click, bad click, right-click, double-click... everything is recorded. If you move your mouse too fast and race through a series of steps, the resulting video will play back the cursor speed in real time. Move too slowly, and your learners will tear their collective hair out as they watch the cursor slowly move across the screen.

In the steps that follow, you'll select a recording area and then record the process of changing the Page Orientation in Notepad or TextEdit.

> **Note:** While Camtasia 2019 is very similar on the Mac and PC, recording screen actions is very different. On the PC, there's a separate program used for recording videos called Camtasia Recorder 2018. On the Mac, you can record videos with Camtasia but there isn't a Recorder 2018 program to start. Because recording videos in the two platforms is so different, I've split the process into two groups. PC users, your activities appear below. Mac users, skip ahead to page 42 for your activities.

Student Activity: Set PC Recording Options

1. Start the Camtasia Recorder 2018 tool. (It can be started like any other application.)

   There are two main things to notice on your display. First, there is a green, dashed box that is likely the size of your display (meaning it's really big). Second, there is a Recorder control panel containing four menus (Capture, Effects, Tools, and Help). There are two main groups on the control panel (**Select area** and **Recorded inputs**). Last, there's a large, red **rec** button.

   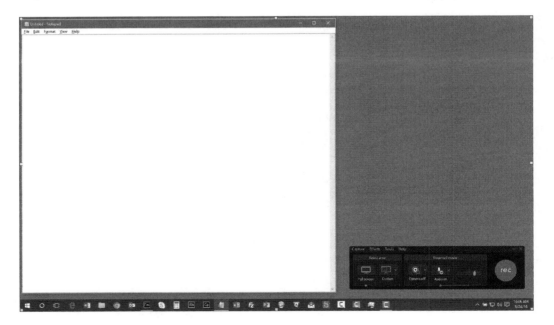

2. Select the Capture File format and File options.

   ☐ on the Recorder control panel, choose **Tools > Options**

The Tools Options dialog box opens.

☐ ensure that the **General** tab is selected

☐ from the **Saving** area, **Record to** drop-down menu, ensure **.trec** is selected (it is selected by default)

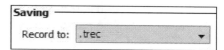

A **trec** file is the default Camtasia recording file format. It's a proprietary file format that can be opened only with Camtasia. Generally speaking, this format works very well with Camtasia.

☐ at the right of the dialog box, click the **File options** button

☐ from the **Output file name** area, select **Automatic file name** (if necessary, this option is the default and is likely already selected)

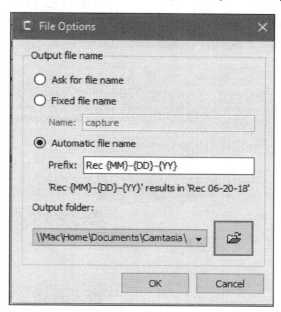

With the **Automatic file name** option selected, you won't be prompted to name the video when you are finished recording. Instead, the recording will automatically be named, saved (by default, recordings are saved to your Documents folder inside a Camtasia Studio folder), and imported into the Camtasia Editor where it can be previewed.

☐ click the **OK** button

3. Select the Capture options.

☐ still working on the **General** tab, ensure your Capture settings match the picture below

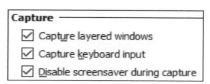

Here is what the **Capture** options do (if you have additional options not shown in the image above, you can leave them as is):

Capture layered windows. On by default. You will be able to capture translucent or irregularly shaped layered windows.

Capture keyboard input. On by default. If you are using the trec file format, Camtasia Recorder captures keys as you press them on your keyboard and automatically creates callouts for you. The callouts can be edited, deleted, moved and resized in Camtasia during production.

Disable screen saver during capture. On by default. You should enable this option when you are creating long, unmonitored recordings.

4. Select the Program options.

☐ with the Tools Options dialog box open, select the **Program** tab

☐ ensure your options match the picture below

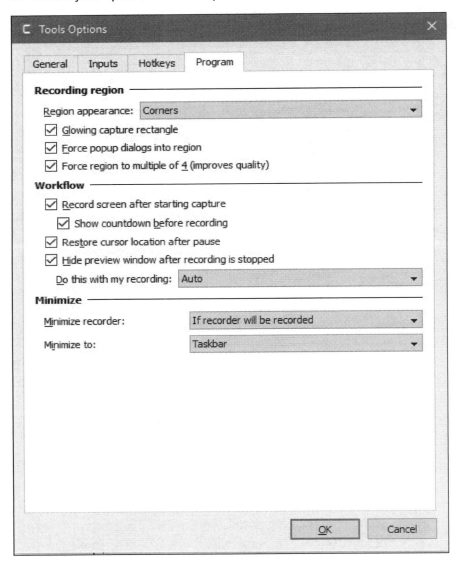

Here is what some of the options do (you can always refer to the Help menu for more information).

Glowing capture rectangle. On by default. Makes the green corners around the recording area flash.

Force popup dialogs into region. On by default. Ensures dialog boxes and other popup windows appear within the recording area.

Force region to multiple of 4. On by default. Prevents errors when viewing videos created with codecs, such as Microsoft Video 1.

Record screen after starting capture and **Show countdown before recording.** Both on by default. Once you click the red **rec** button, the capture process begins. However, you'll have a few seconds to get ready, thanks to a countdown you will see just before the recording begins.

Restore cursor location after pause. On by default. Restores the cursor to the position on the screen prior to the pause. This allows you to seamlessly continue the action in the recording prior to the pause. You must press [**F9**] to pause and resume the recording to use this option.

Hide preview window after recording is stopped. On by default. Select this option if you don't want to preview the captured video after recording.

Minimize recorder. This prevents Camtasia from creating a video of itself.

Minimize to. By default, the recorder will be minimized to your Taskbar if it's going to be in your way during the recording process.

5. Set the Record/Pause Shortcut.

   ❑ with the Tools Options dialog box open, select the **Shortcuts** tab

   ❑ click the **Restore defaults** button

   ❑ from the list at the left, select the **Record/Pause** option

   ❑ from the drop-down menu at the right, notice that **F9** is selected

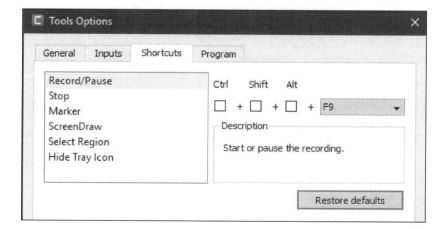

6. Set the Stop Hotkey.

❑ select the **Stop** option from the list at the left

❑ from the drop-down menu at the right, ensure **F10** is selected

The remaining Hotkeys, although important, won't impact the video you are about to create. Understanding that [**F9**] starts or pauses the recording process and that [**F10**] stops the recording process is important to keep in mind for the activity that follows.

❑ click the **OK** button

7. Disable your camera and microphone.

❑ on the Recorder control panel, choose **Capture** and ensure that both **Record audio** and **Record webcam** are **deselected**

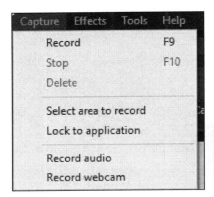 

I'm a fan of including audio in eLearning. In my experience, voiceover audio almost always enhances the learner experience. However, I'm not necessarily a fan of recording audio *during* the video creation process with the Camtasia Recorder. It's not that you can't record quality audio. The concern is that unless you've done a fair amount of recording work, you'll likely end up replacing the audio later in Camtasia. When teamed with the concentration needed to capture screen actions, most people tend to talk too fast, too slow, or flub the recording too much to record decent audio. You'll learn later that it's easy to import, record, and edit audio from within Camtasia (refer to the lessons beginning on page 85).

What about capturing yourself with your video camera? Nope, I'm not a fan of that either. If you're considering capturing video of yourself, ask yourself this question: "Is it really necessary to insert myself into the lesson?" The answer will likely be no. If you do elect to record yourself (recording yourself is often referred to as creating a selfie-video), are you sure you're dressed appropriately? Yes? Okay, but what about what's behind you? Is there a poster in the background that's appropriate? If you look good and the background is great, what about the lighting around you? What about your camera angle (is the camera pointed straight up your nose?)? Because there's much to think about when it comes to selfie-videos, consider not doing them. Also, if you already have awesome videos of yourself, you can insert them into Camtasia later (see page 52).

But enough about recording audio and video. Let's go ahead and record your first software demonstration.

Student Activity: Select a PC Recording Area

1. The Camtasia Recorder should be running. In addition, the Notepad window should be open.

2. Select a recording area.

   ☐ on the **Recorder** control panel, **Select area** section, ensure **Full screen** is selected

   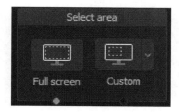

   Full screen means that the recording area is set to record your entire screen. However, unless you are recording a very large application, smaller recording sizes are usually preferred.

   ☐ on the **Recorder** control panel, click the word **Custom**

   The Select area expands and displays a Dimensions box.

   ☐ from the middle of the Recording area, drag the four-headed arrow over to the Notepad window (dragging the four-headed arrow allows you to position the Recording area anywhere you want on your display)

   ☐ on the Recorder control panel, **Dimensions** area, click the **Lock** tool to **unlock** Aspect Ratio

   With this option disabled, you will be able to easily resize the Recording area as you see fit... but keep in mind it is advisable to select Standard recording sizes such as you'll find in the **Custom** drop-down menu (such as 1024x768 or 800x600).

   ☐ resize the Notepad window to any size you like

☐ resize the Recording area so that the entire Notepad window is within the Recording area

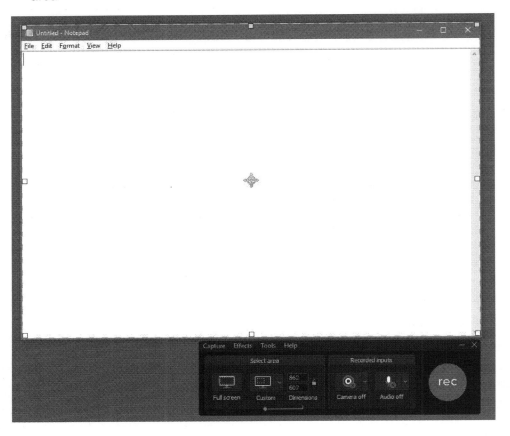

And now, on with the recording!

Student Activity: Record a PC Software Demonstration

1. Record a software demonstration.

   ☐ on the Recorder control panel, click the red **rec** button

   You'll see a three-second countdown.

   ☐ before the counter gets to zero, position your mouse pointer in the center of the Notepad window

   After the counter disappears, your every move (and the time it takes you to move) is being recorded.

   ☐ moving steadily (not too fast), move your mouse pointer to the **File** menu

   ☐ click the **Page Setup** menu item

   ☐ from the **Orientation** area, click **Landscape**

   ☐ click the **OK** button

   ☐ click the **File** menu

   ☐ click the **Page Setup** menu item

   ☐ click the **Portrait** orientation button

   ☐ click the **OK** button

2. Stop the recording process.

   ☐ press [**F10**] on your keyboard

   Once you press the Stop recording hotkey on your keyboard, the recording process terminates and several things happen in rapid succession. First, the Camtasia Recorder application automatically closes. Second, the Camtasia Editor starts and a new project is automatically created. Last, the video you just created is automatically added to the Camtasia Media Bin and inserted onto the Timeline.

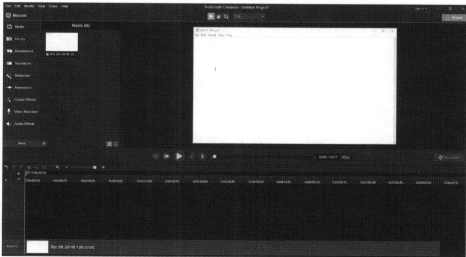

If you'd like to watch the video you recorded, you can use the controls on the Canvas to play and rewind the video.

3. View the location of the recording.

❑ on the **Media Bin**, right-click the recording and choose **Open File Location**

The Camtasia folder opens automatically. By default, all of the recordings you create are saved to this folder. You can change this location in the Camtasia Recorder via **Tools > Options > General > File options**.

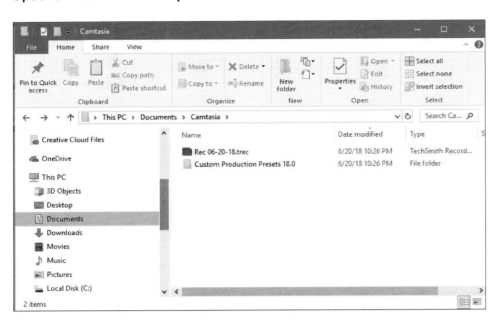

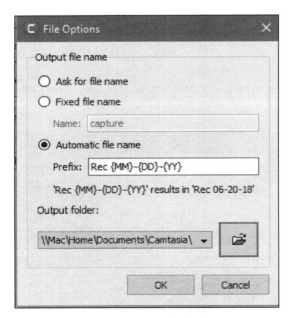

4. Close the window and return to the Camtasia project.

Annotations

Annotations (informational text) can automatically be added to a Camtasia video during the recording process. There are two types of Annotation: System Stamp and Caption. Camtasia can insert one of two system stamps (time/date and elapsed time) into the recording. The stamp is imprinted into the video background (it can never be removed) and is always visible to learners. Captions are frequently used to include a copyright notice or other text message that you want to appear on the video.

Student Activity: Add a Stamp and Caption to PC Videos

1. Ensure that you are working within the untitled Camtasia project you created during the last activity.

2. Start the Recorder from within Camtasia.

   ☐ from the top left of the **Editor**, click **Record**

   The Camtasia Recorder reopens. The Recorder typically remembers your last settings so unless you closed Notepad, the application should be showing within the Recording Area.

3. Add a System Stamp.

   ☐ on the Recorder control panel, choose **Effects > Options**

   The Effects Options dialog box opens.

   ☐ on the **Annotation** tab, select **Time/date**

   ☐ if necessary, deselect **Elapsed time**

   A preview of the date and time format appears just below the check boxes.

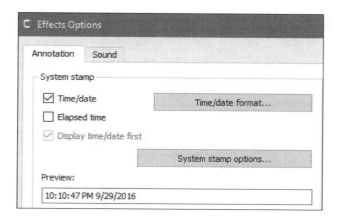

4. Specify a Time/Date Format.

☐ click the **Time/date format** button

☐ from the Display area, select **Date only**

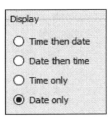

☐ click the **OK** button to return to the Effects Options dialog box

5. Set the System Stamp font.

☐ working on the **Annotation** tab, click the **System stamp options** button

The System Stamp Options dialog box opens.

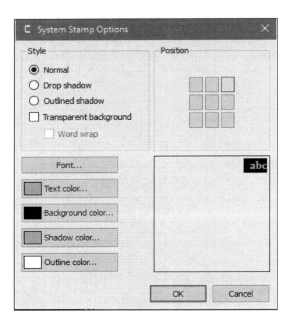

☐ click the **Font** button

☐ change the Font to **Verdana** and the Size to **10**

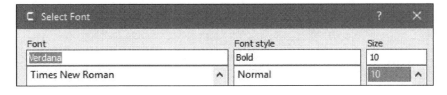

☐ click the **OK** button

You are returned to the System Stamp Options dialog box.

6. Set the System Stamp position.

    ❑ from the **Position** area in the upper right of the dialog box, select the lower left square (this will position the System Stamp in the lower left of the video)

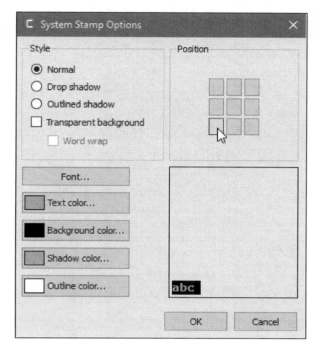

    ❑ click the **OK** button

    You should now be back in the Effects Options dialog box.

7. Add a Caption.

    ❑ click in the Caption text field and type: **This is a sample lesson. Not for resale.**

    ❑ deselect **Prompt before capture**

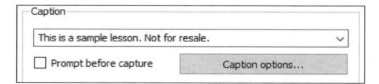

8. Set the Caption font.

    ❑ click the **Caption options** button

    The Caption Options dialog box appears.

    ❑ click the **Font** button

    ❑ change the Font to **Verdana** and the Size to **10**

    ❑ click the **OK** button

9. Set the Caption Text and Background color.

☐ click the **Text color** button

The Select color dialog box opens.

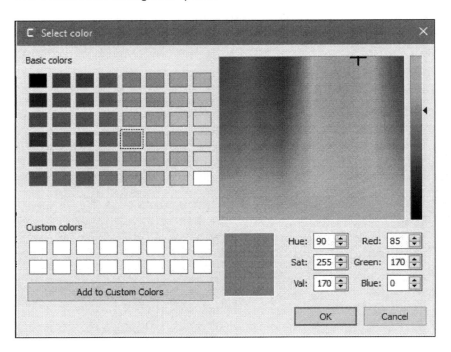

☐ select any color you like

☐ click the **OK** button

☐ click the **Background color** button

The Select color dialog box opens again.

☐ select any color you like

☐ click the **OK** button

10. Set the Caption position.

☐ from the Position area, select the upper right square (this positions the Caption in the upper right of the video)

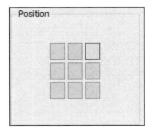

☐ click the **OK** button twice (to close both open dialog boxes)

11. Enable the System Stamp and Caption effects.

    ☐ on the Camtasia Recorder, choose **Effects > Annotation > Add system stamp**

    ☐ on the Camtasia Recorder, choose **Effects > Annotation > Add caption**

    Both commands should now be selected (there should be a check mark next to both).

PC Recording Confidence Check

1. Click the **rec** button on the Recorder control panel.

2. Record the process of changing the page orientation like you did during your first recording session.

3. When finished, stop the recording process.

    Your new recording will be added to the Camtasia Media Bin.

4. Double-click the new recording to open a preview window.

5. Play the preview and notice that you can see both a System Stamp and Caption on the video.

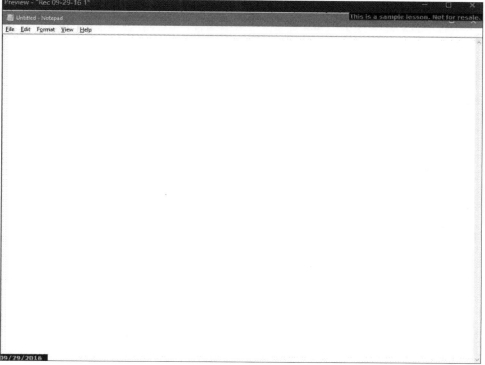

6. Close the preview window.

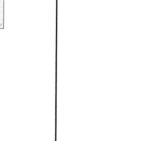

Recording Effects

Starting in the next module, you will learn how to use the Editor to add all kinds of media to an eLearning lesson that will help grab the learner's attention including text, images, and music. However, using Camtasia's Effects Toolbar, you can add several attention-grabbing visuals while you are recording your video. **Note:** If you record effects (as shown below) they are imprinted into the video background like Stamps and can *never be removed from the video*.

Student Activity: Add Effects While Recording on the PC

1. Ensure the Effects toolbar is enabled.

   ❑ from the top left of the Editor, click **Record**

   The Camtasia Recorder reopens.

   ❑ on the **Recorder control panel**, choose **Effects > Annotation** and turn off both Add system stamp and Add captions

   ❑ on the **Recorder control panel**, choose **Tools > Recording toolbars**

   ❑ select **Statistics**, **Effects**, and **Duration**

   ❑ click the **OK** button

2. Record a video and add screen drawings.

   ❑ click the **rec** button

   After the 3-2-1 countdown, the Statistics, Effects, and Duration tools should appear on the Recording toolbar (on some of my systems, the tools appear on their own; on others, I had to click in the middle of the Recording toolbar to coax the tools to appear... you may have to play with this a bit to display the tools).

   ❑ select the **ScreenDraw** tool

   Drawing tools appear. You can select from among frames, lines, highlights, and a pen.

❑ select any of the tools and draw some shapes within the Notepad window

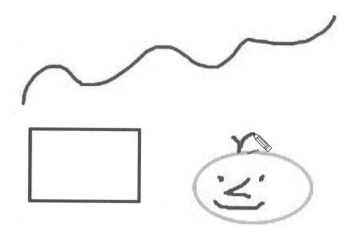

On the Recorder control panel, notice that there are also **Duration** and **Statistic** counters.

❑ when finished drawing, stop the recording

3. Preview the video in Camtasia.

4. When finished, exit Camtasia (there is no need to save the untitled project).

5. Close the Notepad application.

Note: The rest of this modules is for Mac users only. PC users, you can skip ahead to the next module.

Student Activity: Set Mac Recording Options

1. Change Camtasia's Preferences so that you are prompted to save after every recording.

   ☐ from within **Camtasia**, choose **Camtasia 2019 > Preferences**

   The General dialog box opens.

   ☐ click **Recording**

   ☐ from the **After recording** area, choose **Prompt to Save**

   With the **Prompt to Save** option selected, you will be prompted to name the video when you are finished recording and select a Save destination.

   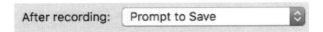

2. Change the Preferences so that recordings are not automatically deleted.

   ☐ from the **Save recordings to** area, remove the check mark from **Delete after**

   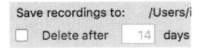

   With **Delete after** disabled, older recordings won't be automatically deleted by Camtasia.

   The remaining Recording options should match the image below.

   In my opinion, the two most important default Preferences that you did not change are **Capture Frame Rate** and **Show countdown before recording**.

By default, recordings are captured at 30 frames-per-second (fps). The higher the frame rate, the smoother a recorded video will be. However, when captured at a high frame rate, the file size of a video can be huge (especially if you record for more than a few minutes). If you find that your videos are excessive, you can experiment with lowering the frame rate here prior to recording (which will lower the size of your recording, but could also lower the quality of the video).

Having the **Show countdown** option turned on is a good default. Without this option enabled, the recording process will begin the instant you click the Start Recording button... so fast you'll possibly find yourself unprepared and make mistakes while recording.

❑ close the Recording dialog box

Student Activity: Select a Mac Recording Area

1. Create a new recording.

   ☐ from within Camtasia 2019, choose **File > New Recording**

   The Camtasia Recorder opens and there is a large green box that is likely surrounding your entire display. The green box is known as the Recording area. You will next change the Recording area's size and select a specific area.

2. Set a recording size and select a recording area.

   ☐ on the **Camtasia Recorder**, click the **first drop-down menu** at the left (shown circled in the image above) and choose **720p HD (1280x720)**

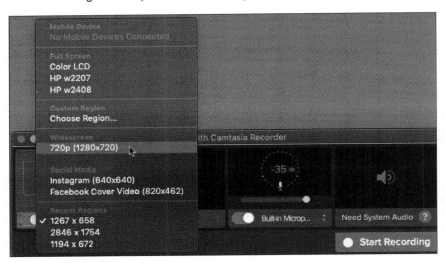

   The recording area is now a green, dashed line. You can now specify any area of your screen as the Recording Area. In this instance, the Recording Area you need is the TextEdit application (its menu bar and application window).

   Note: If you have a small screen, 1280x720 may be too large of a recording area. You can manually resize the capture area to any size that works best (via a corner resize handle like the one shown in the image at the right).

☐ drag the **middle** of the Recording Area so that the upper left of the area begins in the TextEdit menu bar similar to the image below

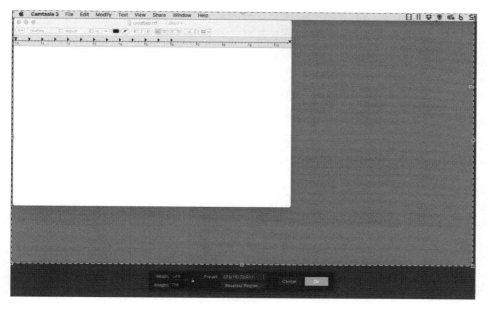

Note: You might find the step above a bit clunky because there is no visual drag area anywhere in the Recording Area. However, dragging the middle of the entire area does allow you to reposition the Recording Area without resizing it. When repositioning the Recording Area, note the appearance of your mouse cursor. You're looking for a hand icon as shown below (indicating that you are moving the Recording Area, not resizing it).

☐ click the **OK** button

3. Ensure the TextEdit window size and the Recording Area match.

❑ resize the TextEdit window as necessary so that the TextEdit window fits nicely within the Camtasia Recording Area

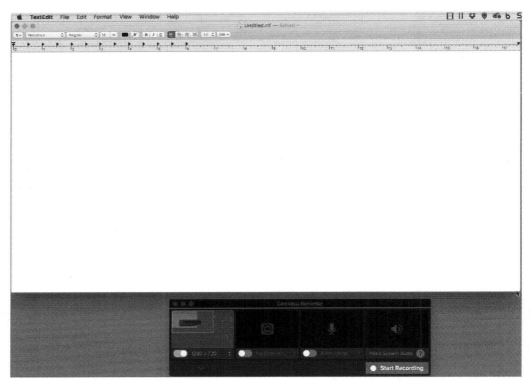

4. Disable the Camtasia Recorder camera and microphone.

❑ on the Camtasia Recorder, deselect both the camera and microphone (if the options are gray, you don't have either a camera or a microphone connected to your computer)

I'm a fan of including voiceover audio in eLearning. In my experience, voiceover audio almost always enhances the learner experience. The dilemma you might face is whether you should record the audio and the video at the same time or add the audio to the video later.

If you are creating micro-learning (very short videos used as "just-in-time learning"), you might want the more informal, natural feel of audio narration recorded while you click through a software process. On the other hand, if you are creating a longer, more formal course, you may want a more formal sound. In this case, I would encourage you to either hire professional talent or record your own voice in a studio and with high-quality equipment.

With some practice, you can record your voice with the Camtasia Recorder while you're creating the video. Or you can record your voice in the Camtasia Editor while you are producing the video. (You will learn how to record and edit audio in Camtasia beginning on page 85). You can also record your voice separately, using any number of audio editing tools (such as Audacity, Sound Forge, or Adobe Audition) and import the audio files into the Camtasia Media Bin.

What about capturing yourself with your video camera? I'm not a fan of that. Ask yourself this question: "Is it really necessary to insert myself into this lesson?" The answer will likely be no. If you do elect to record yourself, are you sure you're dressed appropriately? Yes? Okay, but what about what's behind you? Is there a poster in the background that's inappropriate? If you look good and the background is great, what about the lighting around you? What about your camera angle? Because there's much to consider when it comes to self-videos, consider not doing them. Besides, if you have awesome existing videos of yourself, you can insert them into Camtasia later (see page 52).

But enough about all that. Let's go ahead and record your first software demonstration.

Student Activity: Record a Mac Software Demonstration

1. Record a software demonstration.

   ☐ on the Camtasia Recorder, click the red **Start Recording** button

   You'll see a three-second countdown.

   ☐ before the counter gets to zero, position your mouse pointer in the center of the TextEdit window

   After the counter disappears, your every move (and the time it takes you to move) is being recorded.

   ☐ moving steadily (not too fast), move your mouse pointer to the **File** menu

   ☐ click the **Page Setup** menu item

   ☐ from the **Orientation** area, click **Landscape**

   ☐ click the **OK** button

   ☐ click the **File** menu

   ☐ click the **Page Setup** menu item

   ☐ click the **Portrait** orientation button

   ☐ click the **OK** button

2. Stop the recording process.

   ☐ press [**command**] [**option**] [**2**] on your keyboard

   Once you press the Stop recording hotkeys on your keyboard, the recording process terminates and you are prompted to save the recording.

   ☐ navigate to **Camtasia2019Data > Video_Files**

   ☐ name the recording **Change Page Orientation**

Save Camtasia Recording
Save As: Change Page Orientation ⌃
Tags:
▦⌄   📁 Video_Files ⌄
Name
📄 CreateNewFolderVideo.trec
📄 DeleteFolder.trec
📄 RenameFolderVideo.trec
📄 RestoreFolder.trec

   ☐ click the **Save** button

3. Close the Camtasia Recorder.

4. Import a recording into a new Camtasia project.

❑ from within Camtasia, choose **File > New Project**

❑ from the **left side** of the Camtasia window, click **Media** (to open the Media Bin)

❑ on the **Media Bin**, click **Import Media**

❑ navigate to **Camtasia2019Data > Video_Files**

This is where you should have saved the video you just recorded. In addition to your video, there are other videos that support upcoming modules in this book. Notice that the videos have a **trec** extension which is a TechSmith proprietary format. These **trec** video files can be imported into the Camtasia Editor and used to produce eLearning content. However, **trec** files cannot be shared, opened, or used by other media players.

❑ select **Change Page Orientation.trec**

❑ click the **Import** button

The asset appears on the Media Bin.

5. Add a video to the Timeline and preview the video.

❑ on the **Media Bin**, right-click the video you just imported and choose **Add to Timeline at Playhead** (if your mouse does not support right-clicking, you can press [**control**] on your keyboard and **click** your mouse to see **Add to Timeline at Playhead**)

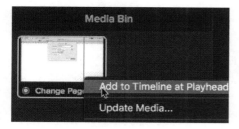

The video is added to a track on the Timeline. And notice that the Canvas now includes a preview of your recording.

☐ on the **Canvas**, click the **Play** tool

If you are unhappy with your first recording, the good news is that it's free to create more. All you'd need to do is click the **Record** tool in the upper left of the Camtasia window or choose **File > New Recording**.

6. Close the Camtasia project (there is no need to save it).

Mac Recording Confidence Check

1. Record a new software demonstration of anything you'd like to record on your computer. (For instance, use your web browser to add a Favorite; change the appearance of text in your word processor of choice, or edit the appearance of an image in your favorite image editor.)

2. When finished recording, save the recording to **Camtasia2019Data > Video_Files** with any name you like.

3. In Camtasia, create a new project and import your new video to the Media Bin.

4. Add the new Media Bin asset to the Timeline and then preview the video.

5. Close the Camtasia project (there is no need to save it).

iCONLOGiC

"Skills and Drills" Learning

Module 3: Adding Media

In This Module You Will Learn About:

- Videos, page 52
- Images, page 58
- Multi-Track Projects, page 60
- Cursor Effects, page 64

And You Will Learn To:

- Import a Video to the Media Bin, page 52
- Add a Video to the Timeline, page 54
- Import Images, page 58
- Add a Track, page 60
- Create a Watermark, page 63
- Add Cursor Effects, page 64

Videos

During the first module of this book, you were introduced to the tools that make up Camtasia, opened a Camtasia project, and explored the Editor interface (page 12). Then you used Camtasia Recorder to record screen actions (beginning on page 31). Now you'll create an eLearning lesson from scratch using the Camtasia Editor.

The first thing you will learn to add to the new Camtasia project is video. When it comes to importing video files, you can import any of the following video formats:

- ☐ **trec** (a recording created with the Camtasia Recorder)
- ☐ **camrec** (a recording created with older versions of the Camtasia Recorder)
- ☐ **mp4** or **mpeg** (a file format created by the Moving Picture Experts Group, which was designed to compress video into a digital format)
- ☐ **avi** (Audio Video Interleave, an early Microsoft video file format), wmv (Windows Media Video developed by Microsoft)
- ☐ **mov** (Apple's proprietary format that plays using only Apple's "Quick Time" player).

Student Activity: Import a Video to the Media Bin

1. Start Camtasia (if necessary).

2. On the **Welcome window**, click **New Project** or, if a Camtasia project is already open, choose **File > New Project**

3. Import a video.

   - ☐ from the top left of the Editor, click **Media** to display the Media Bin
   - ☐ on the **Media Bin** panel, ensure you are in **Thumbnail** view

   - ☐ click **Import Media**

The Open dialog box appears. Any supported video file you can access from your computer can be imported using this dialog box.

☐ from the **Camtasia2019Data** folder, open the **Video_Files** folder

☐ open **CreateNewFolderVideo**

The video appears in the Media Bin.

You will learn later in this book (page 106) that a Camtasia project needs to be rendered (otherwise known as publishing or sharing) so that it can be used by your learners. If you were to render or share the project now, the video on the Media Bin would *not* be included in the shared video. If you intend for imported media to be included in a finished eLearning video, you need to ensure that the media is added to the Timeline. Let's do that next.

These next two steps are for PC users only (Mac users can move to the next activity).

4. Preview the imported video.

☐ on the **Media Bin**, double-click the video you just imported

The imported video opens in a Preview window.

5. Close the preview window. (Leave the Camtasia project open.)

Student Activity: Add a Video to the Timeline

1. Add a video to the Timeline.

   ☐ on the **Media Bin**, right-click the video and choose **Add to Timeline at Playhead**

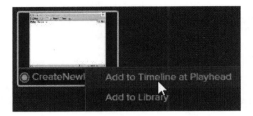

On the Timeline, the video you added is represented by a horizontal bar.

Now that there is an asset on the Timeline, if you share your project so it can be accessed by your learners (page 106), there would actually be something for them to see. And because you have content on the Timeline, you can take advantage of the preview options via the Canvas.

2. Preview a project on the Canvas.

   ☐ on the **Canvas**, click the **Play** button to see the video again

The video plays just like it did via the Preview window. However, there's also an object that moves along the Timeline and it's synchronized with the preview. This object is known as the **Playhead**. You'll spend plenty of time working with the Playhead later.

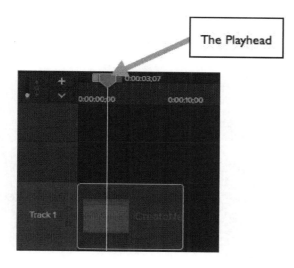

3. Save the project.

   ☐ choose **File > Save**

   ☐ name the project **CreateNewFolder** (ensure you are saving to **Camtasia2019Data**, **Projects** folder) and then click the **Save** button

PC users only: A dialog box appears with some essential messages that are often overlooked. First of all, a Camtasia project contains a **tscproj** extension. Second, these kinds of projects can be opened only with Camtasia. Third, you are reminded that you must produce your video if you'd like learners to be able to use it (something you will learn to do later). Notice that there is a **Don't show again** check box. This is one of those times where getting rid of a dialog box might be a good idea. If you can remember that you'll need to produce your videos before anyone can use them, there is no need to acknowledge this dialog box in the future.

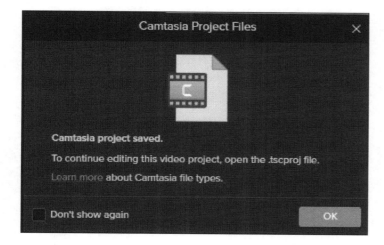

   ☐ **PC users only**: if you'd like, select **Don't show again**

   ☐ **PC users only**: click the **OK** button

Note: You can reset any **Do not show this again** check boxes by choosing **Edit > Preferences** and, on the **Advanced** tab, selecting **Show all tip dialogs** from the **Tips** area.

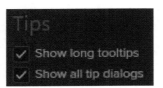

4. All users: On the **title bar** of the Camtasia Editor, notice that the saved project has a **tscproj** extension if you're a PC user; cmproj if you're a Mac user.

At the left, Camtasia for PC users and the tscproj extension. Projects on the Mac get a cmproj extension.

If I were going to give you a pop quiz right about now, a couple of questions you might come across would be about extensions for Camtasia assets. During the past few modules, you have learned that videos created with Camtasia Recorder have a trec extension; and you've learned that Camtasia projects have either a tscproj or cmproj extension. Got it? (There's no quiz coming up by the way... so breathe easy.)

Video Confidence Check

1. Ensure that the **CreateNewFolder** project is open.

2. On the **Timeline**, right-click the video you just added and choose **Delete**.

   The video is removed from the Timeline. Now that it has been removed from the Timeline, it would no longer appear in a produced lesson. However, notice that the video remains in the Media Bin. Items in the Media Bin remain available for you to preview and add to the Timeline, but items in the Media Bin will not appear in a produced video unless they have been added to the Timeline.

3. Ensure the **Playhead** is positioned as far left of the Timeline as it will go.

4. Right-click the video in the Media Bin and choose **Add to Timeline at Playhead** to add the video to the Timeline again.

5. On the Timeline, zoom closer to the video in Track 1 by clicking the **Zoom timeline in** tool.

   The ability to Zoom closer to Timeline objects will prove useful later when you need to split the audio or synchronize the video with other Timeline objects. You can always use the **Zoom timeline out** tool to move farther away from the Timeline or drag the slider (the circle between the plus and minus signs).

6. Save the project (choose **File > Save** or press **[ctrl] [s]**/PC or **[cmd] [s]**/Mac on your keyboard).

Images

Few things enhance an eLearning lesson better than quality images. Camtasia supports many of the standard graphic formats, including bitmaps, GIFs, and JPEGs. You can learn about the different graphic formats with a quick Internet search (one site that I find helpful is **Dan's Data** (www.dansdata.com/graphics.htm). If you don't have ready access to photographs and other images, I've had great success with BigStockPhoto.com and iStockPhoto.com. Both of these sites offer awesome collections of inexpensive, royalty-free images. You'll also find some wonderful eLearning assets on the eLearning Brothers website (www.elearningbrothers.com).

Student Activity: Import Images

1. Open an existing Camtasia project.

   ☐ choose **File > Open Project**

   ☐ open **Camtasia2019Data**

   ☐ from the **Projects** folder, open **ImageMe**

   This project is identical to the one you were just working on. It has the CreateNewFolderVideo in the Media Bin and on the Timeline.

2. Import an image to the Media Bin.

   ☐ choose **File > Import > Media**

   ☐ from the **Camtasia2019Data** folder, open the **Image_Files** folder

   ☐ open **logo.png**

   The logo image appears in the Media Bin.

3. Import another image.

   ☐ choose **File > Import > Media**

   ☐ from the **Image_Files** folder, open **mainart.jpg**

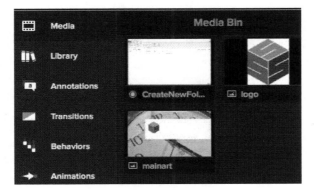

Timeline Confidence Check

1. On the **Timeline**, drag the **CreateNewFolder** video to the **right** approximately one-half inch (this leaves space to the left of the video for the mainart image).

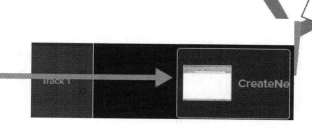

> Drag the Timeline object to the right to make room for other track items at the left.

2. Drag the **mainart** image from the Media Bin to the beginning of Track 1 on the Timeline.

3. On the Timeline, drag the **CreateNewFolder** object **left** until it bumps up against the mainart image).

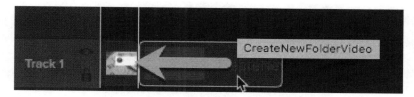

4. On the **Canvas**, click the **Play** button to preview the project.

   Notice that the mainart image appears on the Canvas and then, after a few seconds, the image disappears and the video showing how to create a new folder plays.

   If you want to have one Timeline object appear, then disappear, and then another Timeline object appear, all you have to do is add objects to the Timeline horizontally and move them (or stretch them) on the Timeline to control when they appear and for how long. However, if you want to have multiple Timeline items appear at one time, you'll need multiple Timeline tracks... something you'll learn about next.

5. Save your work.

Multi-Track Projects

You've added two assets to the Timeline (the video and the mainart image). Both objects appear on a single Track called Track 1. You can easily add additional tracks to the Timeline. Once you have multiple tracks, you can precisely control when multiple Timeline objects appear on the Canvas and how items appear on the Canvas in relationship to other Timeline items. For instance, you can add your corporate logo to a Timeline track above the video track and create a watermark effect... perfect for corporate branding.

Student Activity: Add a Track

1. Ensure that the **ImageMe** project is open.

2. Insert a new track.

   ☐ on the top left of the Timeline, click **Add a track**

   On the Timeline, notice that Track 2 has been added above Track 1. Because Track 2 is above Track 1 on the Timeline, anything you add to Track 2 appears to float (stacked) above anything on Track 1 when viewed on the Canvas.

3. Add an image to the Track 2.

   ☐ if necessary, drag the Playhead **left** to the **beginning** of the Timeline

   ☐ on the Media Bin, right-click **logo.png** and choose **Add to Timeline at Playhead**

   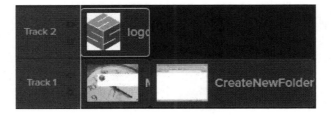

   Only one object can be positioned on a track at a particular time point on the Timeline. Because the Playhead is positioned at 0.00 time and there is an object on Track 1 at that

time point, the logo is automatically added to the next available track (in this instance, the beginning of Track 2). If you hadn't manually added the second track prior to adding the image to the Timeline, the track would have been added automatically.

4. Change when the logo appears on the Timeline.

   ☐ on **Track 2**, position your mouse pointer in the **middle** of the **logo**

   ☐ **drag** the **logo right** until its **left edge** lines up with the left edge of the CreateNewFolder on Track 1

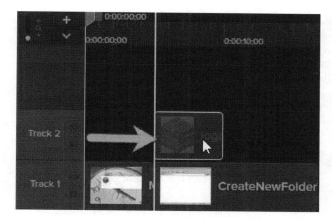

5. Position the Playhead and preview a portion of the video.

   ☐ on the **Timeline**, double-click the CreateNewFolder **video** object

   The Playhead, which indicates the current frame selected (or time point) on the Timeline, should now be positioned just before the CreateNewFolder video.

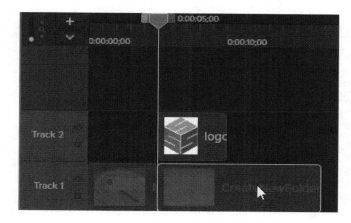

   ☐ on the **Canvas**, click **Play**

   On the Canvas, notice that the logo image appears in the middle of the video by default. In addition, the logo disappears long before the video is finished.

6. Save your work.

NOTES

7. Extend the play time for the logo.

❏ on the Timeline, use your mouse to point to the **right edge** of the logo object

Note: If you are very close to the Timeline, it might be helpful to zoom out a bit before working with the Timeline objects.

❏ when your mouse pointer changes to a **double-headed arrow**, drag the **right** edge of the logo object **right** until the logo's bar ends when the video ends (as shown in the images below)

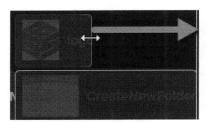

8. Preview the timing changes.

❏ on the Timeline, double-click the **CreateNewFolder** video object

On the Timeline, the Playhead should once again appear just before the **CreateNewFolder** video on the Timeline.

❏ on the **Canvas**, click the **Play** button to preview the project

On the Canvas, notice that the logo image sticks around for the duration of the video. (It's too big, and it doesn't work all that well in the middle of the video... but you'll fix those issues next.)

9. Save your work.

Student Activity: Create a Watermark

1. Ensure that the **ImageMe** project is open.

2. Display the Properties panel.

   ☐ on Track 2, right-click the **logo** and choose **Show Properties** (if you see **Hide Properties** instead, you can move to the next step)

   At the **right side** of the Editor, notice that there's a Properties panel.

3. Make the logo smaller.

   ☐ on the **Properties** panel, drag the **Scale** slider **left** to change the Scale to **50%** (if you find it difficult to get to exactly 50, type **50** into the Scale field at the right)

4. Lower the Opacity of the logo.

   ☐ on the **Properties** panel, drag the **Opacity** slider **left** to change the Opacity to **40%** (again, if you find it difficult to get to exactly 40, type **40** into the field at the right)

5. Change the object's video position.

   ☐ on the Canvas, drag the logo near the bottom right of the background

6. Save your work.

Cursor Effects

Earlier in this module you added a video to the project that demonstrates the process of creating a new folder on a computer (page 52). You've previewed that video several times during this module, so it's likely that you have already noticed that in the video the mouse, through the process of creating a new folder, moves from one part of the window to the next. As the cursor moves, there are no click sounds or visual effects to draw the learner's attention to the clicks. Unfortunately, you're working with an existing video, so there's no way to alter the cursor's behavior... or is there? Because the video was created with the Camtasia Recorder, and it's a .trec file, the cursor can be modified in the Editor (you can easily add such enhancements as click effects and click sounds).

The ability to alter the cursor properties in the Camtasia Editor is an exclusive feature available only in trec and camrec videos created by the Camtasia Recorder. If you import any other type of video into the Editor (such as an mp4 video), you cannot modify the cursor properties.

Student Activity: Add Cursor Effects

1. Open an existing project.

   ☐ choose **File > Open Project**

   ☐ open **Camtasia2019Data > Projects > MouseMe**

2. Preview the lesson.

   ☐ on the **Timeline**, double-click the **CreateNewFolder** video to move the Playhead to the beginning of the video

   ☐ on the **Canvas**, click the **Play** button to preview the project

   As the video plays, pay particular attention to the mouse cursor. It's moving around the screen okay but its path could be a bit smoother. During the steps that follow, you'll smooth out the mouse path and add a visual effect.

3. Smooth the cursor path.

   ☐ on the **Timeline**, double-click the **CreateNewFolder** object to both select and move the Playhead to the beginning of the video

   ☐ from the list of tools at the left, click **Cursor Effects**

   ☐ select the **first icon** (Add highlight, magnifying, or spotlight effect to cursor)

   ☐ right-click **Cursor Smoothing** and choose **Add to Selected Media**

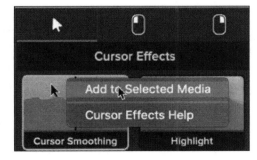

4. Add a Highlight effect to the cursor in the video.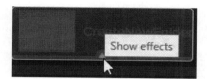

    ☐ from the **Cursor Effects**, right-click **Cursor Highlight** (**Highlight** on the Mac) and choose **Add to Selected Media**

Two effects have been added to the selected video on the Timeline. You can confirm video effects (and delete them) via to the **Show effects** arrow beneath the video object on the Timeline.

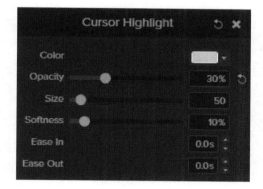

5. Preview the video.

    ☐ on the **Canvas**, click the **Play** button to preview the video

The mouse path is now a bit smoother and you've also added a nifty highlight effect. *How cool is that?*

Note: You can control the appearance of most effects via the **Properties** panel at the right of the Canvas. In the image below, I changed the Opacity of my highlight to 30%, making it easier to see the text behind the highlight.

Cursor Effects Confidence Check

1. On the Timeline, click **Show effects** just below the video.

2. With the effects showing, right-click the **Cursor Highlight** effect and choose **Delete** (**Remove Effect** on the Mac) to delete it.

Note: It's possible to delete the video accidentally instead of the effect. When deleting the effect, ensure that you right-click the effect, not the video itself.

3. Spend a few moments adding different effects to the video's cursor.

4. Experiment with the **Left Click** effects on the Cursor Effects panel.

5. Preview the video to see your new cursor effects.

6. When finished, save your work. (Mac users: You can close all open projects.)

iCONLOGiC
"Skills and Drills" Learning

Module 4: Groups, Annotations, Behaviors, and Transitions

In This Module You Will Learn About:

And You Will Learn To:

Groups

As you continue to add more and more media to the Timeline things are likely to get a bit, shall we say, frenzied. You can have several Timeline tracks, and each track can contain multiple objects. Because you can use the Timeline to precisely control how long each item appears on screen, changing the timing of one object can easily foul up its relationship to objects on other tracks. Given how complex Timeline relationships can become, you'll appreciate Camtasia's ability to group objects. Rather than moving an individual object on the Timeline (only to realize you left a related object on a different track behind), you can group objects and move everything in the group at one time.

Student Activity: Create a Group

1. Open **AnnotateMe** from the **Camtasia2019Data** Projects folder.

2. Move a Timeline object.

   ☐ on the Timeline, drag the **logo** object to the right by 5 or 10 seconds

   After moving the logo, notice that the CreateNewFolderVideo object does not move. Given that these two objects should appear onscreen together, it would be better to group them prior to moving either one of them.

3. Undo the last step.

   ☐ choose **Edit > Undo** (or press [**ctrl** or **command**] [**z**])

   The logo should return to its original Timeline position.

4. Create a group.

   ☐ on the Timeline, select the **CreateNewFolder** video in Track 1

   ☐ press [**shift**] and select the **logo** in Track 2 (then release [**shift**])

   Both the video and the logo should now be selected.

   ☐ right-click either of the selected objects and choose **Group**

   The objects have now been grouped. The logo, which was in Track 2, has been moved into the new group on Track 1.

In the first image above, notice that groups on the PC contain **media**; groups on the Mac contain **clips**. Other than this minor difference in naming conventions, grouping works the same on both platforms.

5. Name a group.

    ❏ right-click the group and choose **Rename Group**

    The group's default name, Group 1, is selected.

    ❏ change the group's name to **Creating Folders** and press [**enter**]

6. Extend the Duration of the mainart image again.

    ❏ on the Timeline, drag the group **right** until its left edge lines up with the **30 second** mark on the Timeline

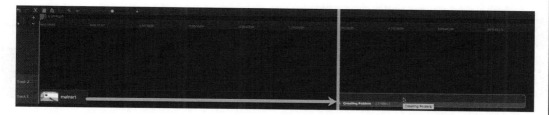

    This time the entire group moves right on the Track leaving a sizable gap between the mainart object and the group. You'll be adding media within the gap shortly.

7. Remove an empty track.

    ❏ at the left of the Timeline, right-click the words **Track 2** and choose **Remove Track**

    Note: Empty tracks do no harm and it is never a requirement to remove them.

    To ungroup objects, right-click a group and choose **Ungroup**. If you'd like to see the objects that make up a group, click the **plus sign** in the upper left of a group to expand the entire group.

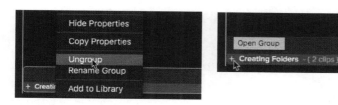

Closing an open group is different on the Mac and PC. After opening a group (by clicking the plus sign), closing or collapsing a group on the PC is as simple as clicking the minus sign (Close group) just above the open group as shown in the image at the left. On the Mac, there's no such icon above the group. Instead, an extra panel has been added to the Timeline. You'll need to click the X to close the group.

Annotations

There are several types of Annotations, including Callouts (shapes that can contain text), Arrows, Lines, Shapes, Motions, and Keystroke Callouts. In the Demo project you opened at the beginning of this book, there are several Callouts synchronized with the voiceover audio. One of the Callouts from that project is shown in the image below (the words CREATE and FOLDERS). During the activities that follow, you will add and then format a few Callouts.

Student Activity: Add a Callout

1. Ensure that the **AnnotateMe** project is open.

2. Insert a Callout.

    ❏ on the Timeline, double-click the **mainart** image to move the Playhead to the far left of the Timeline

    ❏ from the list of tools at the left, click **Annotations**

    The Annotations panel opens.

    ❏ on the **Annotations** panel, click **Callouts** (the first Annotation type)

    ❏ from the **Style** drop-down menu, choose **Basic**

    ❏ right-click the **white rectangle with the black text** and choose **Add to Timeline at Playhead**

3. Remove a Callout's border.

☐ with the Callout selected on the Canvas, open the **Properties** panel (if necessary)

☐ at the top of the **Properties** panel, click **Annotation Properties**

☐ change the **Thickness** to **0** (you can either type a 0 into the field or drag the slider as far left as it will go)

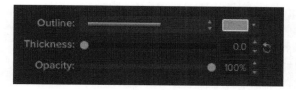

4. Format the Callout's text.

☐ with the Callout still selected on the Canvas, click **Text Properties**

☐ change the Font to **Verdana**

☐ change the text color to **Black**

☐ change the Font size to **80**

☐ change the **Alignment** to **Left**

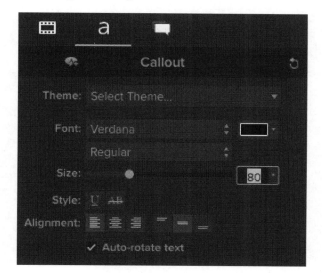

5. Remove a Callout's Drop Shadow.

☐ with the Callout still selected on the Canvas, click **Visual Properties**

☐ click the **X** to remove the Drop Shadow

6. Add the Callout text.

☐ stretch the callout so that is about as wide as the white area within the mainart image

☐ replace the existing text in the Callout with the words **CREATE FOLDERS**

☐ resize and position the Callout on the Canvas similar to the image below

7. Save your work.

Themes

When adding Annotations to the Timeline, it's a good bet that you'll want the appearance of the new objects to be consistent across the entire project. Themes can contain such formatting options as object colors and fonts. Once you've created a Theme, you can quickly apply them to selected objects.

Student Activity: Create and Apply a Theme

1. Ensure that the **AnnotateMe** project is open.

2. Add a second Callout.

   ❑ on the **Timeline**, double-click the **mainart** image to move the Playhead to the **far left** of the Timeline

   ❑ from the **Annotations** tools, click **Callouts** (Annotations are found among the tools at the left; **Callouts** is the first Annotation type)

   ❑ from the **Style** drop-down menu, choose **Basic**

   ❑ right-click the **white rectangle with the black text** and choose **Add to Timeline at Playhead**

   Your new Callout is using default formatting and looks nothing like your first Callout.

3. Apply a Theme to an object.

   ❑ with the newest Callout selected, click either **Text** or **Annotation** on the **Properties** panel

   ❑ from the **Themes** drop-down menu, choose **Default**

While Themes do not contain all of the options available on the Properties panel, the font formatting and background color of the selected Callout change to reflect the properties of the Default Theme.

4. Create a new Theme.

    ❏ with the newest Callout selected, click either **Text** or **Annotation** on the **Properties** panel

    ❏ from the **Themes** drop-down menu, choose **Manage Themes**

    The Theme Manager opens.

    ❏ from the **Theme** drop-down menu, choose **Create New Theme**

    ❏ name the new Theme **SSS Theme**

    ❏ click the **OK** button

5. Set the SSS Theme's Font.

    ❏ from within the **Theme Manager**, click **Fonts**

    ❏ change **Font 1** to **Verdana**

6. Set the SSS Theme's Colors.

    ☐ from within the **Theme Manager**, click **Colors**

    ☐ change the **Foreground** color to **Black** (this controls the color of the text in the Callout)

    ☐ change the **Background1** color to **White**

    ☐ change the **Annotation Background** to **Background1**

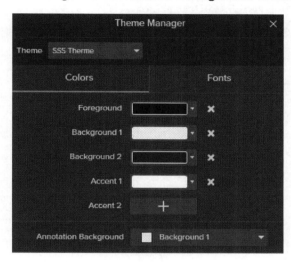

    ☐ click the **OK** button

7. Apply Themes to multiple Callouts.

    ☐ select both of the Callouts you've added so far (selecting one and [**shift**]-**clicking** the second one works great)

    ☐ from the **Themes** drop-down menu on the **Properties** panel, choose **Default**

    Both callouts take on the attributes of the Default Theme.

    ☐ with both callouts selected, choose **SSS Theme** from the **Themes** drop-down menu

    Both Callouts take on the attributes of the SSS Theme you created. If you've created object styles in other programs then this behavior will be familiar to you. Themes are new to Camtasia and the feature is limited. You cannot currently control most of an object's Properties with a Theme (such as border thickness, color, drop shadows, and more). I'm hopeful that as Camtasia continues to be updated by TechSmith, more and more formatting power will be added to the Themes feature.

8. Delete just the second callout you added.

Student Activity: Apply Image Color to Callout Text

1. Ensure that the **AnnotateMe** project is open.

2. In the Callout, highlight the word **CREATE**.

3. Pick up color from an image and apply it to selected text.

   ☐ at the top of the **Properties** panel, click **Text Properties**

   ☐ from the color area, select the **Select color from image** tool

   ☐ using the **Select color from image** tool, click the green "S" on the logo

   The color you clicked with the **Select color from image** tool is applied to the highlighted text in the Callout.

4. Save your work.

Callouts Confidence Check

1. Click in front of the word **FOLDERS** and press [**enter**].

2. Press [spacebar] a few times to indent the word **FOLDERS**.

3. It's likely that the font size changed a bit. If you'd like, make the font it a bit larger.

4. On the Timeline, right-click the Callout and **Copy** it to the clipboard.

5. On the Timeline, position the Playhead just to the right of the Callout.

6. **Right-click** the existing Callout and choose **Paste**.

   Drag the newest callout so it is positioned just after the first callout in Track 2.

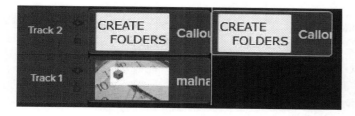

7. Double-click the new Callout and change the word **CREATE** to **RENAME**.

RENAME
FOLDERS

8. On the Timeline, position the Playhead just to the right of the second Callout.

9. **Right-click** the Callout and choose **Paste**.

10. Drag the newest callout so it is positioned just after the second callout in Track 2.

11. Drag the new Callout up against the second Callout.

12. Double-click the new Callout and change the word **CREATE** to **DELETE**.

NOTES

13. Change the word **FOLDERS** to **RESTORE**.

14. Save your work.

15. Create a **new** Camtasia project.

16. Spend a few moments adding some of the other Annotations to the project. (There is no need to save the new project so feel free to play as much as you'd like.)

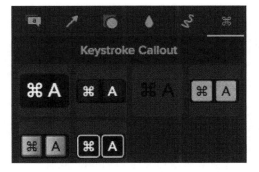

As you add the Annotations, notice the formatting options available to you on the Properties panel. You'll find that the options vary depending upon the type of Annotation you're working with.

Behaviors

Behaviors, also known as Effects, are animations that are typically used to add some visual excitement to your project. Behaviors can be attached to images, video clips, and several types of Annotations. A Behavior can be added to a single object or stacked together with other Behaviors to create unique effects.

Student Activity: Add a Behavior to a Callout

1. Open **BehaveMe** from the **Camtasia2019Data** Projects folder.

   The BehaveMe project is similar to the AnnotateMe project you closed a few moments ago except it has some additional Callouts added to Tracks 2 and 3. In particular, notice the three ampersands (**&**) added to Track 2 at 10;05, 15;18, and 20;18.

   The stacking order on the Timeline is important. Notice that each ampersand is **behind** the Callouts you added earlier. The stacking effect was easily attained by placing the ampersand in a lower track. In the image above, the **DELETE RESTORE** Callout is in Track 3; the ampersand is in Track 2. Objects in higher tracks are positioned above objects in lower tracks. In the next step, you'll be adding a Behavior to the ampersands.

2. Add a Behavior to a Callout.

   ☐ on Track 2, double-click the first **ampersand** positioned at **10;05** to highlight it on the Canvas

   ☐ from the list of tools at the left, click **Behaviors**

   ☐ right-click **Jump And Fall** and choose **Add to Selected Media**

The Jump and Fall effect is added to the Callout and appears below the Timeline object. It can be removed by right-clicking the effect and choosing **Delete** (PC) or **Remove Effect** (Mac).

3. Preview the effect.

   ❑ with the Playhead positioned just to the left of the **ampersand** you just altered, click the **Play** button on the Canvas

   The ampersand drops in from the top of the canvas, bounces a few times, and then drops off the bottom of the Canvas.

4. Change the effect's timing.

   ❑ on the **Timeline**, drag the **left edge** of the **ampersand** Callout **right** a few seconds

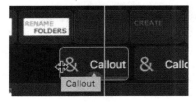

5. Preview the timing change.

   ❑ with the Playhead positioned just to the left of the **RENAME FOLDERS** Callout (the second Callout on Track 2), click the **Play** button on the Canvas

   This time the Callout appears and then, a few seconds later, the animated ampersand does its thing.

6. Modify the Behavior.

   ❑ on Track 2, double-click the **ampersand** you've been working with to highlight it on the Canvas

   Currently, the ampersand drops in from the top of the Canvas. Let's see what other tricks you can make the Callout perform.

❏ on the **Properties** panel, select **Behavior Properties**

❏ from the **Behavior Properties**, select the **In** tab

❏ from the **Style** drop-down menu, choose **Hinge**

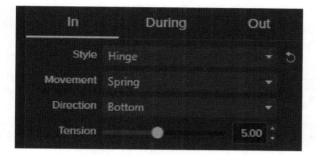

7. Preview the effect.

❏ with the Playhead positioned just to the left of the **ampersand** you just altered, click the **Play** button on the Canvas

This time the ampersand swings up from the bottom of the Canvas.

Behaviors Confidence Check

1. Spend a few moments playing with the **In**, **During**, and **Out** settings available on the **Properties** panel.

2. Add a Behavior to the remaining two ampersands (remember, there are ampersands at Timeline positions **15;18**, and **20;18**).

3. Preview the effects and adjust the timing of the ampersand Callouts as you see fit.

4. Using the Properties panel, adjust the effects as you see fit.

5. Select and then group mainart image and the Callouts (name the group **Introduction to folders**).

6. Save your work.

NOTES

Transitions

You can use Transitions to add a smooth, professional visual break between clips in a project. There are several Transition types available on the Transitions panel, including Glow, Fold, and, my personal favorite, Cube rotate.

Student Activity: Add a Transition to a Group

1. Open **TransitionMe** from the **Camtasia2019Data** > **Projects** folder.

   This project picks up where you left off during the last Confidence Check except I've added a few more grouped assets to the Timeline (such as Get Ready and Lesson 1).

2. Preview a few Transitions.

   ☐ from the panel at the left, click **Transitions**

   ☐ from the list of **Transitions**, hover above **Fade**

   A sample of the Fade Transition appears on the thumbnail.

   ☐ on the **Transitions** panel, hover above the **Wheel** Transition to see a preview

   ☐ on the **Transitions** panel, hover above the **Cube rotate** Transition to see a preview

3. Add a Transition to selected media.

   ☐ on the **Timeline**, select the **Get Ready** group

   ☐ on the **Transitions** panel, right-click the **Cube rotate** Transition and choose **Add to Selected Media**

   On the Timeline, a transition has been added to the beginning of the selected group... and it's been added to the beginning of the next group. You can tell that a transition has been added via the green rectangles. The transition was added to the second group (even though you didn't select that group) because, by default, transitions are added to the beginning and end of a selected group and to the beginning of the next group that it is touching.

4. Save your work.

Student Activity: Modify Transition Timing

1. Ensure that the **TransitionMe** project is open.

2. Preview the video from the beginning.

   As the video plays on the Canvas, the Cube rotate transition should appear at the beginning and end of the first clip and again at the beginning of the second clip. It's a cool effect, but you'd like to speed it up a bit.

3. Modify Transition Timing.

   ☐ on the Timeline, drag the first green transition a bit to the left

   ☐ drag the second green transition a bit to the right

4. Preview the video.

   The timing for each transition should be a bit faster than before.

Transitions Confidence Check

1. Working in the **TransitionMe** project, add any Transition you like to each of the groups.

2. Preview the project to see transitions.

3. During the preview, did you notice that the transition between clips isn't quite as smooth as it could be (it's almost as if a tiny part of the clip plays twice)? Try this little trick: right-click the **second and third** transitions and deselect **Use Trimmed Content in Transition**.

4. Repeat the process for the remaining transitions.

5. Preview the project to see smoother transitions.

   In my experience, I only leave **Use Trimmed Content in Transition** selected if I want part of a video to appear across a transition—something I rarely need.

6. Save your work.

Notes

iCONLOGiC
"Skills and Drills" Learning

Module 5: Audio

In This Module You Will Learn About:

- Importing Audio Media, page 86
- Voice Narration, page 91
- Splitting Media, page 95
- Audio Editing, page 99

And You Will Learn To:

- Add Background Music From the Library, page 86
- Fade Audio In, page 89
- Record Voice Narration, page 92
- Split a Music Clip, page 95
- Rename Tracks, page 99
- Silence and Cut Audio, page 100

Importing Audio Media

When you import audio media into a Camtasia project, the following formats can be imported: WAV, MP3, M4A, and WMA.

WAV (WAVE): WAV files are one of the original digital audio standards. These kinds of files, while of extremely high quality, can be very large. In fact, typical WAV audio files can easily take up to several megabytes of storage per minute of playing time. If you have a slow Internet connection, download times for files that large are unacceptable.

MP3 (MPEG Audio Layer III): MP3 files are compressed digital audio files. File sizes in this format are typically 90 percent smaller than WAV files.

M4A: M4A (MPEG 4 Audio): M4A files are similar to MP3 files. They are smaller than WAV files but of excellent quality and could one day replace MP3s.

WMA (Windows Media Audio): WMA is a popular audio format developed by Microsoft. WMA files are often smaller than MP3 files.

Student Activity: Add Background Music From the Library

1. Open **AudioMe** from the **Camtasia2019Data** Projects folder.

2. Add background music to the project from the Library.

   ☐ from the list of tools at the left, click **Library**

   ☐ open the **Music Tracks** folder

   ☐ right-click any of the audio files in the Music Tracks folder and choose **Add to Timeline at Playhead**

The audio file appears on the Timeline in Track 2 as a series of sharp lines—a waveform.

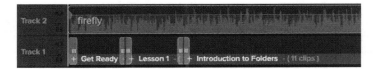

3. On the Canvas, Play the first part of the video to hear the background music.

Library Audio Confidence Check

1. On the Timeline select and delete the background music you just added from the Library.

2. On the Media Bin, notice that while you've removed the music from the Timeline, a copy of the unused media asset is retained.

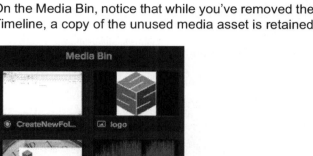

3. On the Library, add a second Music Track to the Timeline.

4. Preview the video to hear the newly added music.

5. On the Timeline select and delete the new background music.

6. On the Media Bin, notice that the newest music is also retained.

   While unused media won't appear in your final, published project, it's a best practice to remove unused project media from time to time. Doing so will ensure that your project's file size is as streamlined as possible.

7. Right-click the Media Bin and choose **Delete Unused Media**.

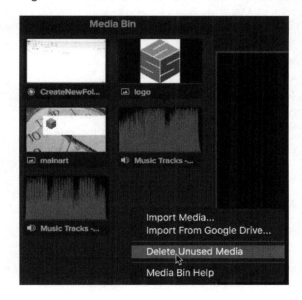

8. Save your work.

Student Activity: Import Background Music

1. Ensure that the **AudioMe** project is open.

2. Import an audio file to the Media Bin.

   ☐ choose **File > Import > Media**

   ☐ navigate to the **Audio_Files** folder within the **Camtasia2019Data** folder

   ☐ open **2Step1.mp3**

   The imported audio clip appears in the Media Bin.

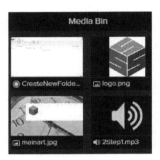

3. Add the imported audio to Track 2.

   ☐ on the Media Bin, right-click **2Step1.mp3** and choose **Add to Timeline at Playhead**

4. Preview the video to hear the background audio you just added to the Timeline.

5. If you listen to the music until the end you'll notice that the audio fades out nicely. However, if you preview the beginning of the video, you'll notice that the audio starts just a bit too abruptly. You will take care of that next when you learn to how to fade music in (or out).

Student Activity: Fade Audio In

1. Ensure that the **AudioMe** project is open.

2. Fade audio in.

   ☐ on the **Timeline**, select the background music on Track 2

   ☐ from the panel at the left, click **Audio Effects**

   ☐ from the **Audio Effects** panel, right-click **Fade In** and choose **Add to Selected Media**

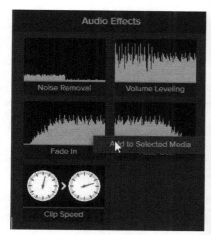 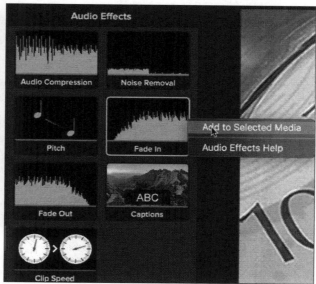

Shown above, the Audio Effects for Camtasia 2019 for Windows; at the right, the Mac version of Camtasia 2019.

Notice that a ramp has been added to the left of the waveform.

The ramp begins at the bottom of the waveform and then gets taller until the audio hits a consistent level. You can manually drag the green line to control how the audio fades in, but you'll probably be happy with the level established automatically by Camtasia.

3. Preview the beginning of the video to hear the fade effect you just added to the audio.

4. If you'd like the fade effect to last a bit longer, drag the green circle on the waveform **right** to extend the fade timing.

Fading Confidence Check

1. Delete the background music from the Timeline.

2. Using the Library, add any Music Track to the Timeline.

3. It's likely that the music that you just added to the Timeline plays far longer than your other Timeline assets. If that's the case, drag the **right side** of the background music **left** until the end of the music lines up with the assets in the last group on the Timeline.

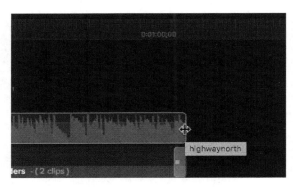

4. Use the **Audio Effects** to add **Fade In** and **Fade Out** effects to the background music you just added to the Timeline as you see fit.

5. Preview your work.

6. Save your work.

Voice Narration

Camtasia allows you to record your own narration and sound effects and add them to any available Audio Track. If you plan to record your own audio, you will first need a microphone connected to your computer. After the microphone, consider the following:

Voiceover Scripts: You saw an example of an eLearning script on page 24. As with a write a step-by-step eLearning script, it's important to include a voiceover script for yourself or your voiceover talent... and rehearse the script as much as possible prior to recording. Rehearsals are the perfect opportunity to find which words in the script, if any, are going to trip up you or the narrator.

Location, Location, Location: Get yourself into a quiet space—consider a "Do Not Disturb" sign on your door. You might be surprised by how much noise there is in an average office. Your microphone will probably pick up every nearby sound. Before using your office or cubicle as your recording studio, take a break and listen. Turn down the ringer volume on your phone. Is the water dripping? Is the printer squeaking? Is your neighbor coughing nonstop?

USB vs. Analog Microphones: You can use either type of microphone when you record your audio. However, you'll probably get better results using a USB microphone.

Audio Setup: If you plan to use high-end audio hardware, such as a mixer or preamplifier, plug your microphone into the hardware and then plug the hardware into your computer's "line in" port. Set the volume on your mixer or preamplifier to just under zero (this will minimize distortion).

Microphone Placement: The microphone should be positioned four to six inches from your mouth to reduce the chance that nearby sounds will be recorded. Ideally, you should position the microphone above your nose and pointed down at your mouth. Also, if you position the microphone just to the side of your mouth, you can soften the sound of the letters S and P.

Microphone Technique: It's a good idea to keep a glass of water close and, just before recording, take a drink. To eliminate breathing and lip-smack sounds, turn away from the microphone, take a deep breath, exhale, take another deep breath, open your mouth, turn back toward the microphone, and start speaking. Speak slowly. When recording for the first time, many people race through the content. Take your time.

Monitor Your Audio Level As You Record: When recording your audio, you will see an Input Level meter on Camtasia's Voice Narration panel indicating how well the recording process is going. When the meter is green to yellow, you're fine. However, when the meter is orange to red, you are being warned that you are too close to the microphone or that you are speaking too loudly.

Student Activity: Record Voice Narration

1. Using a word processor, open **CreatingFoldersVoiceoverScript** from the **Other_Assets** folder within the Camtasia2019Data folder.

    Let's pretend for a moment that you've been hired to serve as the voiceover talent for an eLearning project. It's quite possible you'd get a script similar to the file you've just opened.

    > **Audio File 1:**
    > Welcome to Super Simplistic Solutions learning series.
    > This is lesson one: Creating New Folders.
    >
    > **Audio File 2:**
    > This lesson is going to teach you how to create a new folder on your computer, how to rename it, and how to both delete and restore recycled items.
    >
    > **Audio File 3:**
    > When creating folders keep in mind that you can create as many folders as you need.

2. Rehearse the audio script.

    ❏ using a slow, deliberate cadence, read the following out loud:

    Welcome to Super Simplistic Solutions learning series.

    This is lesson one: Creating New Folders.

    Next you'll record your voice in Camtasia. (You can close the script now if you'd like.)

3. Using Camtasia, open **NarrateMe** from the **Camtasia2019Data** Projects folder.

4. Record voiceover audio.

    ❏ on the **Timeline**, position the Playhead on the **Lesson 1** group

    ❏ from the panel at the left, click **Voice Narration**

On the Voice Narration panel, notice that I have already pasted the part of the voiceover script you'll be recording. Alternatively, you could print the script and have it beside you during the recording phase.

☐ if necessary, select **your microphone** from the drop-down menu at the top of the Voice Narration panel

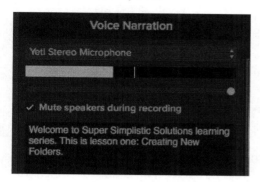

☐ ensure **Mute timeline during recording** is selected

Muting the Timeline is a good idea for this video because you have background audio in Track 2. If you don't mute the audio, it will likely play through your computer speakers and ruin your voiceover audio.

And now... prepare yourself! Once you start the recording process, there isn't a count-down or any kind of warning. Instead, Camtasia simply records your voice. While recording, the video will play on the Canvas so you can see what's happening in your lesson while you narrate.

☐ click the **Start Voice Recording** button

☐ using a slow, deliberate cadence, read the following out loud:

Welcome to Super Simplistic Solutions learning series.

This is lesson one: Creating New Folders.

5. When finished, click the **Stop** button.

Mac users, the audio is automatically saved and added to the Timeline. PC users, the Save Narration As dialog box opens.

☐ PC users only: name the file **My_Lesson1_Voiceover** and save it to the **Audio_Files** folder within the **Camtasia2019Data** folder

All users, your voiceover narration appears on a new track on the Timeline. In addition, the new audio has been added to the Media Bin.

6. Preview the video.

   You should be able to hear your new voiceover audio. However, you should also be concerned that the audio is hard to understand with the background music playing so loudly. You'll fix that shortly.

7. Save your work.

Splitting Media

You will find Camtasia's ability to split media segments on the Timeline to be a valuable feature. Have you imported an audio clip that's too long and difficult to manage? Click at the top of Timeline where you want to split the audio clip and quickly split the clip into as many segments as you need. Want to add a transition in the middle of a video clip? Because transitions cannot be inserted in the middle of a clip, click where you need a transition and insert a split.

Student Activity: Split a Music Clip

1. Open **SplitMe** from the **Camtasia2019Data** Projects folder.

   This is basically the same project you were just working on except the voiceover audio that you recorded and inserted during the last activity has been replaced by professional voiceover audio.

2. Preview the video.

   Notice that the background music and voiceover audio are playing at the same time, making it difficult to understand what the narrator is saying.

   In the steps that follow, you will split the background music into two parts and then manipulate the two audio pieces on the Timeline so that they don't fight with the voiceover audio. During the splitting process, it's possible not only to split the background music but also to inadvertently split media in other tracks. To prevent that you'll need to lock the tracks. To that end, you will lock both tracks 3 and 1. Changes you make to the media in Track 2 (which will remain unlocked) will not accidentally affect media in other tracks.

   When I first learned how to use Camtasia, there were no books to buy and there was little professional training available. Because I am self-taught on how to use the tool, I was never educated about the need to lock certain tracks before editing objects on other tracks. If I highlighted part of a track and deleted a selection, the same selection in unlocked tracks would also be deleted! In one project, I learned my mistake only hours later when previewing the finished video. By then, it was far too late to undo my mistake.

3. Lock Tracks.

   ☐ at the far left of the Timeline, click the padlock icon next to **Track 1** and **Track 3** to **lock** those tracks (only **Track 2** should remain unlocked)

4. Split the background music in Track 2 into two segments.

□ on the top of the Timeline, click at the **4;29** mark to position the Playhead

□ on the Timeline, select the audio in **Track 2**

□ right-click the **Playhead** and choose **Split Selected**

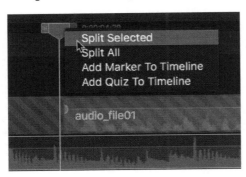

And just like that, the background music has been split into two segments.

Audio Timing Confidence Check

1. Select the second (larger) segment of the background music.

2. Drag the **left edge** of the segment to the right until it lines up with the end of the **audio_file01** media in **Track 3**.

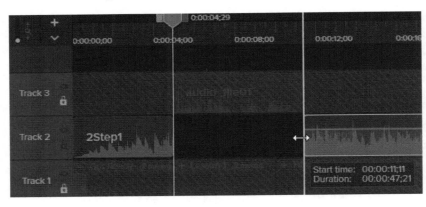

3. Select the **first segment of the background music** and, using the **Audio Effects** panel, **Fade Out** the media.

4. Select the second segment of the background music and **Fade In** the media.

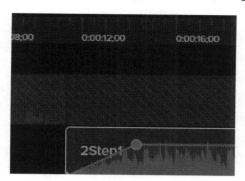

5. Preview the video.

    The background music stops pretty much when the narrator begins to speak. Nice. The music shouldn't start again until after the narrator is finished speaking.

    There's a problem now with the timing for Lesson 1 group. The group isn't on the Canvas quite long enough to match the voiceover audio. To fix that, you'll need to change the timing of a few Timeline objects.

6. On the Timeline, unlock both locked tracks.

7. Select and drag both the **Introduction to Folders** and **Creating Folders** groups right by just a few seconds (leaving room to stretch the Lesson 1 group).

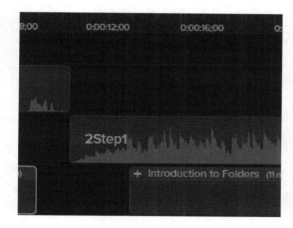

NOTES

8. Stretch the Lesson 1 group right to make its playtime match the voiceover audio in Track 3.

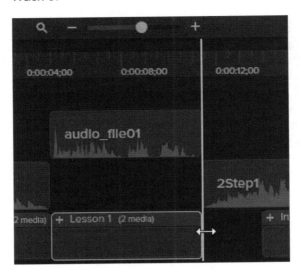

9. Move the Timeline groups as necessary to ensure your Timeline matches the images below.

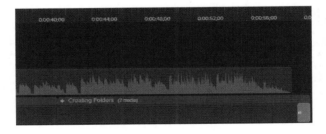

10. Save your work.

Audio Editing

Earlier in this module you learned how to edit an audio clip by fading the volume in and out. Camtasia offers you other editing options such as the ability to cut segments of a waveform and even replace unwanted audio with silence.

Student Activity: Rename Tracks

1. Open **EditMyAudio** from the **Camtasia2019Data** Projects folder.

   This project is similar to the project you were just working on with a few notable exceptions. First, two of the tracks have names that are more descriptive than Track 1, Track 2, etc. (Voiceover and Background Audio).

   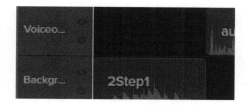

   There's also additional voiceover audio in the Voiceover track.

2. Rename a track.

   ☐ on the far left of the Timeline, double-click the name **Track 1**

   ☐ replace the text with the word **Main** and press **[enter]**

   Naming your tracks is always optional. However, in larger project with more than just a few tracks, I find that naming my tracks makes it easier and more efficient to produce my projects.

Student Activity: Silence and Cut Audio

1. Ensure that the **EditMyAudio** project is open.

2. Preview an audio clip.

   ☐ on the **Timeline**, double-click **audio_file02_silence** and then preview the video

   There are two strange sounds in the clip and there's a bit of dead air at the end of the audio file. You have two choices for removing unwanted audio segments: delete the content or replace the content with **Silence**. When deleting, the duration of the audio clip is reduced by the amount of audio that is deleted. However, if your goal is to simply remove a problem in the audio clip (such as click sounds) without altering the duration of the clip, using Silence is an ideal solution.

   ☐ stop the video

3. Replace a selection of audio with Silence.

   ☐ lock the **Background** and **Main** tracks

   As you learned earlier, locking a track ensures changes made to other unlocked tracks will not effect locked tracks.

   ☐ on the **Voiceover** track, double-click **audio_file02_silence** to position the Playhead at the beginning of the audio file

   ☐ at the top of the **Timeline**, drag the **Zoom** slider right to zoom closer to the Timeline

   At this enhanced view, you can get a better look at the waveform that makes up the audio file. You can see that the narrator's audio levels are consistent across the wave.

   Take a look at about the **15 second** mark on the Timeline. There's a spike in the wave that isn't consistent with the rest of the wave. This part of the wave is an erroneous sound that you need to edit.

   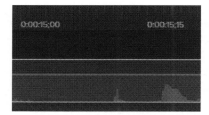

☐ drag the Playhead to the beginning of the errant sound

☐ drag the Playhead's red out point right to highlight the sound

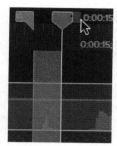

☐ right-click the selection and choose **Silence Audio**

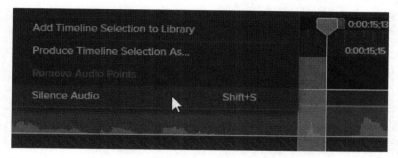

The click sound or whatever it was has been removed without altering the playtime of the media.

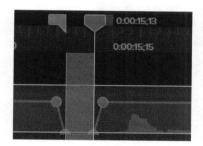

☐ double-click the Playhead to pull the red portion back to its default position (the red box at the right of the Playhead should snap back to the Playhead)

4. Cut audio.

☐ on the Timeline, scroll **right** to the end of the **audio_file02_silence** media

There is a bit of dead air in the audio_file02_silence media that you can delete.

☐ position the Playhead to the left of the last second or so of the **audio_file02_silence** media

☐ drag the Playhead's red out point **right** to select through the end of the media

☐ right-click the selection and choose **Delete** (PC) or **Delete Range** (Mac)

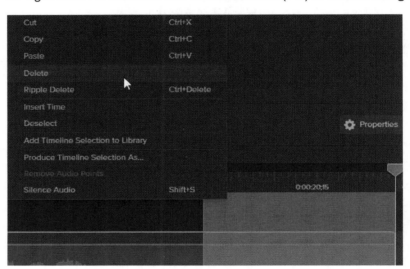

The selected portion of the audio clip is removed leaving a gap on the Timeline. Because the other tracks were locked, the media on those tracks have not been affected.

Audio Editing Confidence Check

1. There's another errant sound at about the 16 second mark on the Timeline.

2. Select and then replace the sound with Silence.

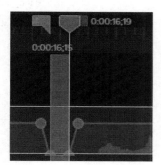

   Note: Remember to double-click the Playhead to return it to its default setting (the red box should snap back to the Playhead).

3. Zoom away from the Timeline far enough so that you can see the gap left on the Timeline when you deleted a portion of the audio media.

4. Drag **audio_file_03 left** to occupy the gap.

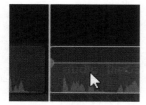

5. Preview the project from the beginning.

6. Save your work.

Notes

iCONLOGiC
"Skills and Drills" Learning

Module 6: Sharing

In This Module You Will Learn About:

- Standalone and Web Videos, page 106

And You Will Learn To:

Standalone and Web Videos

As you have worked through the first several modules in this book, you learned how to record a video using the Recorder (page 33). Then, beginning on page 52, you learned how to add video to the Editor. Then you added images (page 58), Annotations (page 70), Behaviors (page 79), and audio (page 85).

At some point you are going to want to wrap up the development process and render (publish) your project into a format that your learners can use. Keep in mind that to view your published content, learners will not need to purchase or use Camtasia. Instead, learners can view your output (assuming they have access to it) using free tools such as Web browsers or media players that are typically found on their computer out of the box.

Camtasia's Share menu contains several menu items that allow you to quickly Share your finished project. For instance, you can render a standalone video that you can email to a learner. The standalone file can be opened by free video players such as Windows Media Player. You can Share a project so it can be accessed from your internal servers or Learning Management System.

Shared content can be used by learners on devices such as desktop computers, laptops, and mobile devices (smart-phones, tablets, etc.). There are even Share options allowing you to render and then automatically upload your content to Screencast.com, YouTube, Vimeo, or Google Drive.

During the next few activities you'll learn how to share your project as a standalone video and as a video that be accessed via a web browser. The process of creating videos is very different for Mac and PC users. First up, Mac users. PC users can skip ahead to page 111.

Student Activity: Create a Standalone Video on the Mac

1. Open **ShareMe** from the **Camtasia2019Data** Projects folder.

2. Produce the video for the web.

   ☐ choose **Share > Local File**

   The Export As dialog box opens.

   ☐ change the **Export As** name to **Create_Folders_MP4_Only**

   ☐ navigate to the **Produced_Videos** folder (the folder is inside the **Camtasia2019Data** folder)

Export As:	Create_Folders_MP4_Only.mp4	⌄
Tags:		
Where:	📁 Produced_Videos	⇕

   ☐ from the **File format** drop-down menu at the bottom of the dialog box, choose **Export to MP4 (.mp4)**

File format:	Export to MP4 (.mp4) ⇕	Options...

   ☐ click the **Export** button

The project is exported and you'll be able to track its progress during the process via the dialog box shown below. At this point, you won't be able to work within Camtasia without first canceling the export process.

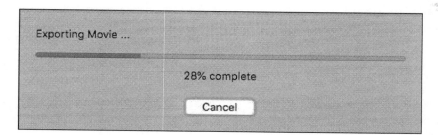

Once the export is complete, you'll see an **Export finished** dialog box.

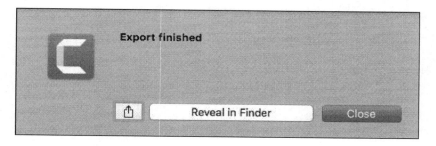

❑ click the **Reveal in Finder** button

The Produced Videos folder opens. The only file in the folder at this point is the single video that you just exported.

3. Open the video file in a media player.

❑ right-click (or [**control**] click) the video and choose **Open With > QuickTime Player.app**

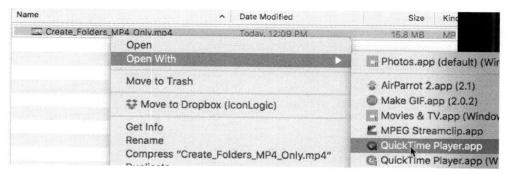

The published video opens.

☐ click the **Play** button on the playbar to start the video

I don't know about you, but I think this whole production process went just a bit too smoothly. I bet you're thinking that I set this project up in advance so that when you produced it things would go perfectly. And I'm betting that you're betting that once you try to do this on your own, the wheel's going to come off the cart and nothing is going to work as smoothly as it just did.

Let me assure you that the production process you just worked through was based on default settings you'll find in Camtasia "out of the box." There was nothing in the ShareMe video set up in advance to ensure success in the Sharing process. In fact, you can run through the production process using any Camtasia project and your result should be similar those shown in this activity.

You will get a chance to play with some of the other Sharing options in a bit. For now, enjoy your progress. Believe it or not, you are now a published eLearning author. Congratulations!

4. Close the media player and return to the Camtasia project.

Student Activity: Export a Mac Project as a Web Page

1. Ensure that the **ShareMe** project is open.

2. Share the video so it will play via a Web browser.

   ☐ choose **Share > Local File**

   ☐ change the **Export as** name to **ShareMe_Web_Version**

   ☐ if necessary, navigate to the **Produced_Videos** folder

   ☐ from the **File format** drop-down menu at the bottom of the dialog box, choose **Export to MP4 (.mp4)**

   ☐ select **Export as Web Page**

   ☑ Export as Web Page   Options...

   ☐ click the **Export** button

   ☐ once the Export is complete, click the **Reveal in Finder** button

   The first time you shared a file, you shared the file as a standalone video. And once it was exported, the process yielded a single file. This time, you've created assets that will rely on each other to correctly open in a browser. Should you upload these assets to your web server, the files must be kept together.

   ☐ open the **ShareMe_Web_Version** folder

   There's single html file in the folder (this is the start page for the lesson) and a media folder.

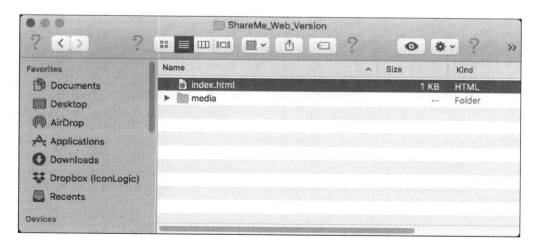

❏ double-click **index.html** to open the page in your default browser

❏ click the **Play** button in the middle of the screen to play the lesson

3. When finished, close the browser window to close the lesson.

4. Return to the Camtasia project.

   The next few activities are for PC users only. You can skip ahead to the "Share to YouTube" section of this book (on page 120).

Student Activity: Create a Standalone Video on the PC

1. Open **ShareMe** from the **Camtasia2019Data** Projects folder.

2. Produce the video for the web.

   ☐ choose **Share > Local File**

   The Production Wizard opens.

   ☐ select **MP4 only (up to 1080p)** from the drop-down menu

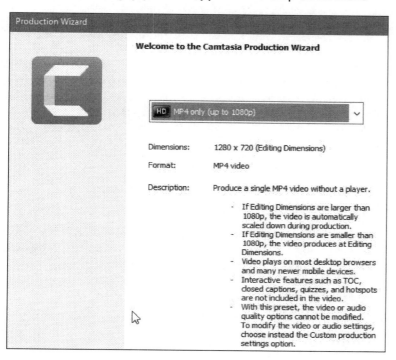

   ☐ click the **Next** button

   The **Where would you like to save your video files(s)?** screen appears.

3. Select a file name and folder.

   ☐ change the **Production name** to **ShareMe_MP4_Only**

   ☐ click the **yellow folder** at the right of the **Folder** drop-down menu and open the **Produced_Videos** folder (the folder is inside **Camtasia2019Data** folder)

   ☐ click the **Save** button

   You should be back in the **Where would you like to save your video files(s)?** window.

☐ ensure the remaining options match the picture below

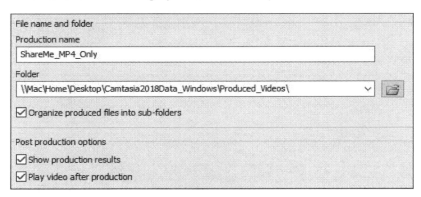

By selecting **Organize produced files into sub-folders** you ensure that the rendered video and its support files are kept together. (Although the video you just produced is a standalone video and does not require support files, other formats that you produce will require several support files.) The two **Post production options**, which you also left selected, show a report of the production process in case there were errors and ensure that your rendered video plays automatically once the rendering process is complete.

4. Render the video.

☐ click the **Finish** button

Your project is rendered. You can track the process on the Rendering Project screen. Generally speaking, the longer your video and the more audio clips you used on the Timeline, the longer the rendering process takes to complete.

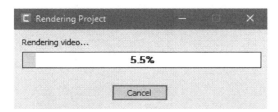

Once the rendering process is complete, the video automatically opens in your default video player and begins to play. In the image below, the video is open in my Windows Media Player.

I don't know about you, but I think this whole production process went just a bit too smoothly. I bet you're thinking that I set this project up in advance so that when you produced it things would go perfectly. And I'm betting that you're betting that once you try to do this on your own, the wheel's going to come off the cart, and nothing is going to work as smoothly as it just did.

Let me assure you that the production process you just worked through was based on default settings you'll find in Camtasia "out of the box." There was nothing in the ShareMe video set up in advance to ensure success in the production process. In fact, you can run through the production process using any Camtasia project, and your result should match those shown in this activity.

You will get a chance to play with some custom Production settings in a bit. For now, enjoy your progress. Believe it or not, you are now a published eLearning author. Congratulations!

5. Review the Production Results.

❑ close the media player

The **Production Results** dialog box contains some important information about your rendered project, including the location of the produced file and the size of the video.

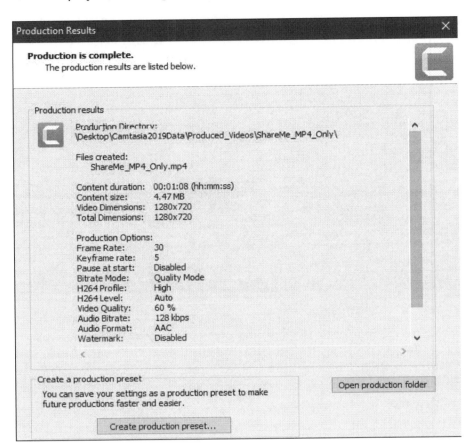

6. View the production files.

❑ click the **Open production folder** button

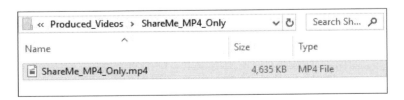

The **ShareMe_MP4_Only** folder opens. This folder contains the lone rendered file you'll need to deliver to your learner.

« Produced_Videos › ShareMe_MP4_Only		
Name	Size	Type
ShareMe_MP4_Only.mp4	4,635 KB	MP4 File

❑ close the **ShareMe_MP4_Only** window

❑ click the **Finish** button on the Production Results dialog box

Student Activity: Create a Web Video on the PC

1. Ensure that the **ShareMe** project is open.

2. Produce a video for the web that includes the Smart Player.

   ☐ choose **Share > Local File**

   The Production Wizard appears again.

   ☐ from the drop-down menu, **MP4 with Smart Player (up to 1080p)**

   ☐ click the **Next** button

   ☐ name the Production file **ShareMe_SmartPlayer**

   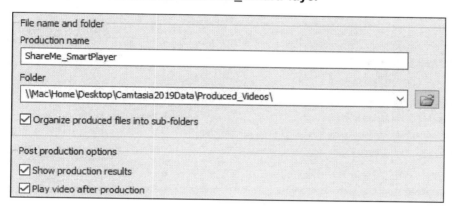

   ☐ click the **Finish** button

   Once rendered, the lesson does not open in the Media Player like last time. This time it opens in your default Web browser.

   ☐ click the **Play** button in the middle of the screen to play the lesson

   The Smart Player appears at the bottom of the window every time you move your mouse within the browser window. The player automatically disappears when you move your mouse away from the browser window.

3. Close the browser window to close the lesson.

4. View the production folder.

☐ from the Production results screen, click the **Open production folder** button

When you published a standalone video, the production folder contained only one file (the MP4 video). Publishing content as web video results in several output files. Because this output is expected to work on desktop computers, laptops, and mobile devices, more files are needed to ensure the content loads correctly in the browser and can remain potentially interactive (interactivity includes such things as quizzes and hotspots which you will learn about later). *All of the files in the output folder are required for the lesson to play/display correctly for your learner.*

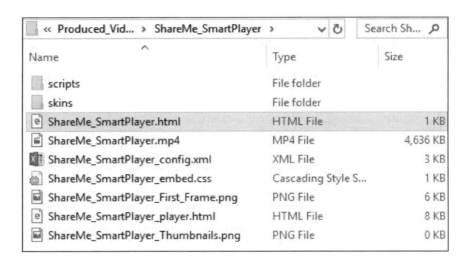

In the image above I've highlighted one of the output files—the *start page*. The start page, which has an html extension, was created automatically when you shared (rendered) the project. The start page is always given the name you type when you render projects. Although all of the files in this folder are co-dependent and must be uploaded to the server, the start page is the page your learners click to start the lesson. If you are working with a webmaster or IT professional, he/she needs to know to not only keep the files together, but to also make the start page the target of any links to the eLearning content.

5. Close the production window.

6. Back in Camtasia, close the Production Results screen by clicking the **Finish** button.

Student Activity: Add a Watermark to PC Projects

1. Ensure that the **ShareMe** project is open.

2. Add a watermark.

   ❏ choose **Share > Local File**

   ❏ select **Custom production settings** from the drop-down menu

   ❏ click the **Next** button

   ❏ ensure that **MP4 - Smart Player (HTML5)** is selected

   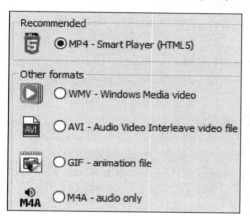

   ❏ click the **Next** button

   Among other things, this second screen allows you to disable the controller (the play bar) if you'd like. You'll leave the default settings.

   ❏ click the **Next** button again

3. Add a watermark.

   ❏ from the **Watermark** area, select **Include watermark**

   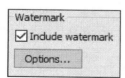

   ❏ click the **Options** button just below Include watermark

   The Watermark options appear along with a Watermark Preview window.

   ❏ click the **Browse** button at the right (the yellow folder)

   ❏ from the **Camtasia2019Data > Image_Files** folder, open **ForReviewOnly**

The image appears, by default, in the lower right of the Watermark Preview.

4. Change the position of the watermark.

   ☐ from the **Position** area, click the **top right** square (you may need to move the Watermark Preview window out of the way to see the Position area)

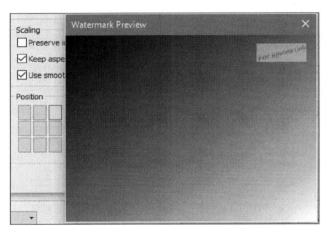

5. Remove a watermark's background color.

   ☐ from the **Effects** area, select **Use transparent color**

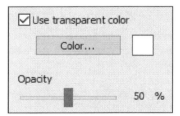

The background color behind the logo has been removed.

6. Change the Image scale.

   ☐ from the **Image scale** area, drag the slider until the scale changes to **30%**

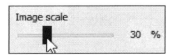

❑ click the **OK** button

❑ click the **Next** button to move to the final screen

7. Give the video a new production name.

❑ change the Production name to **ShareMe_watermark**

Output file
Production name:
ShareMe_watermark
Folder:
\Desktop\Camtasia2019Data\Produced_Videos\

❑ click the **Finish** button

After rendering, the video (including the watermark), opens in your default web browser.

8. Close the browser.

9. Back in Camtasia, close the Production Results dialog box (click the **Finish** button).

10. Save your work.

NOTES

Student Activity: Share to YouTube

1. Ensure that the **ShareMe** project is open.

   Before you can share a video on YouTube, you will need a YouTube account. If you do not already have a YouTube or Gmail account, go to **www.youtube.com** or **gmail.com** now and set one up (it takes only a few moments and is free).

2. Produce a video to be uploaded to YouTube.

   ❑ choose **Share > YouTube**

   The Production Wizard appears again.

   ❑ select **Share to YouTube** from the drop-down menu

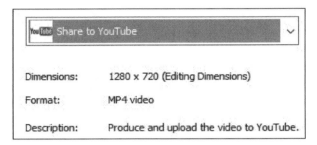

   ❑ click the **Next** button

   You must login to your YouTube account. Once you do, you are taken to the **Produce and Upload to YouTube** screen.

   ❑ click the **Next** button

3. Give the video a Title, Description, and Tags (keywords).

   ❑ in the Title field, type **Creating New Folders**

   ❑ in the Description field, type **This demonstration will teach you how to create a folder using Windows.**

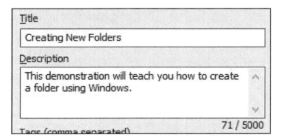

   ❑ in the Tags field, type **training, windows, file management**

   The tags make it easier for YouTube users to search YouTube and find your video.

4. Select a Category.

   ❏ from the Category drop-down menu, select **Education**

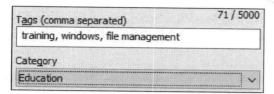

5. Set the Privacy level.

   ❏ from the Privacy area, select a **Privacy** setting

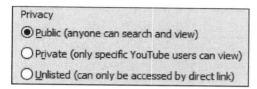

6. Render the video.

   ❏ click the **Finish** button

   The video is rendered again. However, once rendered, it is automatically posted to YouTube.

Sharing Confidence Check

1. If you have a Vimeo account, Share your project to Vimeo.

2. If you have a Google Drive account, Share your project to your drive. (You should be able to use the same account credentials you used for sharing on YouTube.)

If you work with a team of Camtasia developers it's likely that you will be asked to share your project with others (so they can modify the project). Sharing projects between developers is not the same as using the Share menu to render content for your learner. On the Mac, sharing a project with other developers is simple: send a team-member the **cmproj** file and you're set. (The **cmproj** file is a self contained collection of all project assets. If a team-member has the same version of Camtasia as you, they'll be able to open the project without issue.)

If you want to share a Windows-based project with someone who is using Camtasia for the Mac, that's no problem either. Visit the **File** menu and you'll find a menu item named **Export for Windows** if you're on a Mac; **Export for Mac** if you're using Camtasia for Windows.

However, if you want to share a project between Camtasia 2018 PC users, things aren't so simple. In PC projects, assets added to the Media Bin are **linked** to their original location. When you import media into Camtasia from a local or network drive and then send the Camtasia project file to someone outside your network, that person is prompted to locate the linked media before the project opens in his/her copy of Camtasia. It's likely that person will not be able to find those linked assets.

Here's how to get past that problem: *(Note: The final few steps in this Confidence Check are for PC users only. Mac users can skip ahead to the next module.)*

3. PC users only, choose **File > Export as Zip**.

4. Click the yellow folder and select a destination on your computer or network. (Ensure **Include all files from Media Bin in zip** is selected.)

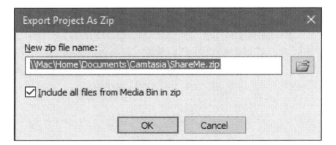

5. Click the **OK** button.

The resulting zip file contains all of your project's assets. You can now share this zip file with fellow Camtasia developers who have everything they need to open and edit the project (assuming they also have Camtasia 2018 or newer installed).

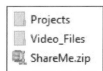

iCONLOGiC

"Skills and Drills" Learning

Module 7: Extending, Zooming, and Hotspots

In This Module You Will Learn About:

- Extending, page 124
- Zoom Animations, page 126
- Markers, page 130
- Hotspots, page 134

And You Will Learn To:

- Extend a Video Frame, page 124
- Add a Zoom-n-Pan Animation on the PC, page 126
- Add a Zoom Animation on the Mac, page 128
- Add a Timeline Marker for a TOC, page 130
- Add an Interactive Hotspot, page 134

Extending

If you record screen actions and then import audio later (as you've done several times during the lessons in this book), synchronizing the screen actions shown in the video with the voiceover audio can be difficult. In those instances where the voiceover audio is referring to something before the event occurs in the video, you'll be happy to learn that you can extend the playtime of a single video frame until the video and the audio catch up to each other.

Student Activity: Extend a Video Frame

1. Open **ExtendZoomMe** from the **Camtasia2019Data** Projects folder.

2. At the **2:26;00 second mark** on the Timeline, notice that **audio_file07** has been added to the Timeline above the **RestoreFolder** video.

3. Position the Playhead at **2:26;00** and **preview** the video.

   The narrator is talking about the Recycle Bin and how much its appearance has changed to indicate there's trash to be emptied. The video is just a bit ahead of the voiceover audio. Rather than re-record the video, you're going to freeze a single frame in the video just long enough to synchronize the voiceover audio with the video.

4. Lock the **Voiceover** and **Background** tracks. (You learned about locking tracks on page 95.)

5. Split a video into two segments.

   ❏ on the **Timeline**, zoom a bit closer to the **2:26;00** mark
   ❏ on the **Timeline**, drag the **Playhead** a bit right to **2:26;16**

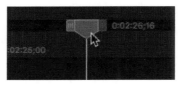

   This is the point in the video just before the cursor moves toward the Recycle Bin.

   ❏ on the **Timeline**, select the **RestoreFolder** media
   ❏ right-click the **Playhead** and choose **Split Selected**

   The video has been split into two segments.

❑ drag the **Playhead** right to **2:29;05**

❑ drag the larger of the two video segments **right** until it snaps at the Playhead's position (at **2:29;05**)

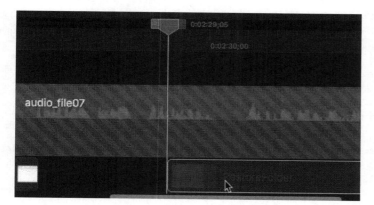

The gap between the two video segments (shown in the image above) is going to be filled with the first segment's last frame. Now you'll extend the frame in the smaller of the two segments. The process of extending a frame is a bit different between the Mac and PC versions of Camtasia. The steps for the Mac appear first, followed by the steps for the PC.

❑ Mac users, leave the **Playhead** positioned at **2:29;05**, select the first part of the split video (the smaller segment) and choose **Edit > Playhead > Extend Frame to Playhead**

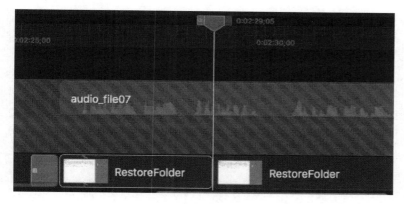

❑ PC users, double-click the smaller video segment, right-click the segment and choose **Extend Frame**

❑ type **2.63** and click the **OK** button

6. Preview the video from the beginning of the first RestoreFolder segment.

Extending the frame has slowed down the video just enough that the screen actions and voiceover audio are pretty well synchronized.

7. Unlock the locked tracks and then save your work.

Zoom Animations

The Zoom-n-Pan feature is useful if the width and height of your project are large and you want to focus the learner's attention on a specific area of the screen. Zooming moves the learner closer to the screen; Panning automatically moves the screen for the learner. Adding Zooms and Pans is as simple as positioning the Playhead where you want to add the effect, accessing the Zoom-n-Pan panel (via Animations) and stretching and/or moving the Zoom-n-Pan window.

Student Activity: Add a Zoom-n-Pan Animation on the PC

1. Ensure that the **ExtendZoomMe** project is open.

2. Add a Zoom-n-Pan mark.

   ☐ on the **Timeline**, position the Playhead at **47;27**

   This is the moment in the video when the mouse pointer has arrived at the Home tab and is about to click.

   ☐ from the list of tools at the left, click **Animations**

   On the PC version of Camtasia, there are two tabs: **Zoom-n-Pan** and **Animations**. On the Mac side, there's just **Animations**. Creating a Zoom effect is very different between the two platforms. Let's tackle the PC side first. Mac users, you can turn to page page 128.

   ☐ PC users, select the **Zoom-n-Pan** tab

   On the **Zoom-n-Pan** panel, notice that there is a box around the entire preview. If left alone, there won't be any zoom or pan effect applied to the video because you haven't yet told Camtasia to do anything to the video at the Playhead's position.

   ☐ on the **Zoom-n-Pan** panel, drag the lower right resizing handle **up** and to the **left** similar to the picture below

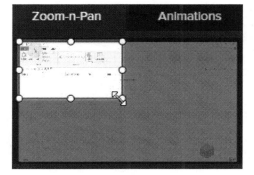

As you drag the resizing handle on the Zoom-n-Pan panel, the effect is automatically added to the video, and you get closer to the Canvas.

On the Timeline, notice that an animation marker (an arrow with a dot at the end) has been added. You can view and edit the Properties of the zoom by clicking the larger dot and observing the Properties panel.

3. Preview the Zoom-n-Pan.

    ☐ on the **Timeline**, position the **Playhead** a few seconds to the left of zoom effect you just added

    ☐ preview the video

    Notice that, thanks to the Zoom-n-Pan feature, you are automatically taken closer to the action on the screen.

4. Save your work.

    The next activity is for Mac users only. PC users can skip ahead to the lessons on Markers, page 130.

Student Activity: Add a Zoom Animation on the Mac

1. Ensure that the **ExtendZoomMe** project is open.

2. Add a Zoom-n-Pan mark.

   ☐ on the **Timeline**, position the Playhead at **47;27**

   This is the area of the video where the mouse pointer has arrived at the Home tab and is about to click.

   ☐ from the list of tools at the left, click **Animations**

   ☐ from the list of Animations, drag **Custom** to the **Creating Folders** group at **47;27** on the Timeline

   ☐ on the Timeline, select the larger circle ◉ ▶ Creating Folders on the animation icon

   The first (smaller) circle represents the beginning of the animation. The second circle represents the end of the animation.

   ☐ on the Properties panel, change the **Scale** to **200**

   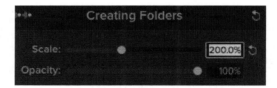

❏ on the **Canvas**, drag the video down and to the right so you can see the top left of the video

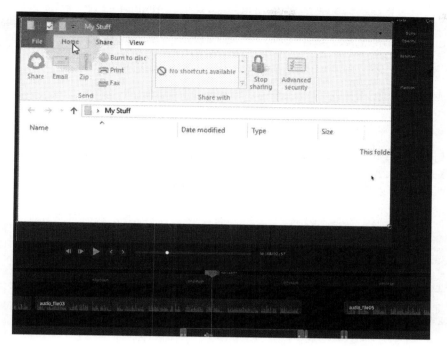

3. Preview the Animation.

❏ on the **Timeline**, position the **Playhead** a few seconds to the left of the zoom Animation you just added

❏ preview the video

Notice that, thanks to the Zoom-n-Pan feature, you are automatically taken closer to the action on the screen.

4. Save your work and close the project.

Markers

In a few moments you will add a table of contents (TOC) to your project and Interactive Hotspots. Markers, which are typically added to the Timeline, can be used to create hyperlinks (jumps) throughout a project. Allowing your learners to jump around a lesson is often referred to as Branching.

Student Activity: Add a Timeline Marker for a TOC

1. Open **MarkMe** from the **Camtasia2019Data** Projects folder.

    Notice that there are new tracks in this project: Nav1, Nav2, and Nav3. These tracks contain simple shapes. Later, you will set things up so that learners will be able to click the shapes to access specific areas of the course (known as markers). You'll add the markers next.

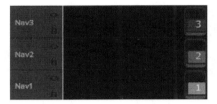

2. Add a Marker.

    ❑ on the **Timeline**, drag the **Playhead** to beginning of the **Get Ready** group

    ❑ choose **Modify > Markers > Add Timeline Marker**

    A marker has been added above the Timeline. On the Properties panel, the new marker is ready to receive a name.

    ❑ on the **Properties** panel, change the **Maker name** to **Home**

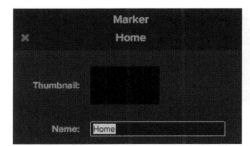

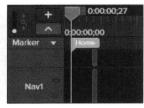

Markers and TOC Confidence Check

1. Still working in the **MarkMe** project, move the Playhead to the beginning of the **Lesson 1** group.

2. Add a new marker (**Modify > Markers > Add Timeline Marker**) named **Lesson 1: Creating New Folders**.

3. Position the Playhead at the **Lesson 2** group.

4. Add a new marker named **Lesson 2: Renaming Folders**.

5. Position the Playhead at the **Lesson 3** group.

6. Add a new marker named **Lesson 3: Recycling and Restoring**.

   The Timeline should now have four markers.

You have learned how to share your projects to YouTube and Vimeo. If you share your project as MP4-only (just a video), it cannot be interactive (no TOC for instance, no interactive hotspots, and no quiz). If you have access to a Learning Management System or web server, you can upload the rendered output files there. But what if you don't have either of those? Where can you upload your content so that it is readily available and, if it contains interactivity, ensure that the interactivity works? Fortunately, TechSmith provides a free service called Screencast where you can test and share your content. The video you are about to work with contains a quiz. You'll upload the video to Screencast.com and be able to test the quiz.

Note: You will need to create a free account on Screencast.com prior to finishing the steps below. If you do not have an account, go to **www.screencast.com** and set one up now.

7. Share the project to **Screencast.com**. (You'll find Screencast in the Share menu.)

8. Title the course **Working_with_Folders**.

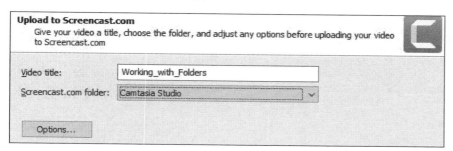

9. **PC users**, click the **Options** button and then select the **Options** tab. Ensure **Table of contents** is selected and click the **OK** button

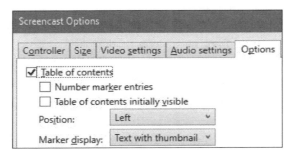

Mac users, deselect **Include Quiz** and ensure **Create table of contents from markers** is selected.

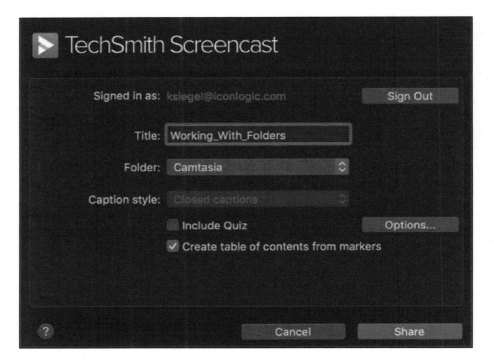

Mac users, click the **Share** button. (You can click the **Visit** button on the **Share History** dialog box to see the lesson on Screencast.com.)

10. **PC users,** click the **Next** button and deselect Report quiz results through email (there is no quiz in the project) and click the **Finish** button

11. Once the project is generated, view it on Screencast.com.

12. **All users:** The Table of Contents can be opened via the icon on the playbar at the bottom of the lesson. If you click the icon, the TOC will open in the upper left of window. You can click any of the thumbnails to jump around the lesson.

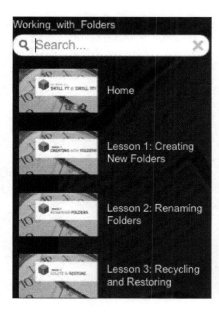

Note: If the TOC does not work for you, try copying the web address in the browser address bar and pasting it into the address bar within a different browser. On my Mac, I found that Chrome worked better than Safari.

13. Close the browser and return to Camtasia.

14. Close all open windows.

15. Save your work. (Mac users, you can save and close any open projects.)

Hotspots

To maximize the effectiveness of your eLearning videos, you can add interactivity via a hotspot. The hotspots you add can allow your learners to jump to specific markers within a video, add links to websites, and more.

Here are the options available to you when you create a Hotspot:

Pause at end: Once clicked, the video stops based on the hotspot's end time on the Timeline.

URL: Takes the learner to a website.

Marker: Takes the learner to a specific marker.

Time: Takes the learner to a specific time in the video.

Student Activity: Add an Interactive Hotspot

1. Open **HotSpotMe** from the **Camtasia2019Data > Projects** folder.

   As mentioned at the beginning of this module, there are three shapes on the Canvas and at the beginning of the project (you can also see them on the Timeline in the **Nav1**, **Nav2**, and **Nav3** tracks). You are going to set it up so if learners click the shapes, they will jump to a specific part of the course. You already created the targets for those jumps when you added the **Home**, **Lesson 1**, **Lesson 2**, and **Lesson 3** markers earlier.

2. Add an Interactive Hotspot to an object on the Canvas.

   ☐ zoom a bit closer to the **Timeline**

   ☐ on the **Timeline**, **Nav1** track, double-click the **green shape**

   The object containing the number **1** is displayed on the Canvas and selected.

   ☐ **PC users**, from the **Tools** panel at the left, click **Annotations** and select **Special** (the one that looks like a water drop); **Mac users**, from the **Tools** panel at the left, click **Visual Effects**

   ☐ **PC users**, right-click **Interactive Hotspot** and choose **Add to Timeline at Playhead**; **Mac users**, right-click **Hotspot** and choose **Add to Selected Media**

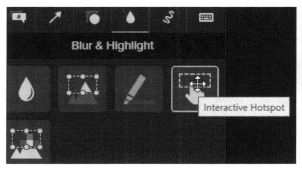

At the left, the Interactive Hotspot tool on the PC; above, the Mac version.

❑ **PC users only**: on the Canvas, position and resize the hotspot over the green shape similar to the image below

3. Add an Action to a Hotspot.

❑ go to the **Properties** panel

❑ from the **Interactive Hotspot** area, ensure **Pause at end** is selected (this ensures that the video doesn't move forward without giving the learner a chance to click)

❑ select **Marker**

❑ from the Marker drop-down menu, choose **Lesson 1: Creating New Folders** (you learned how to create this particular marker on page 130)

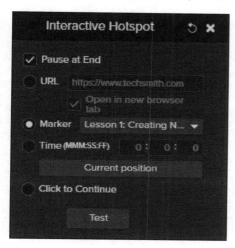

4. Save your work.

Hotspot Confidence Check

1. Add a second Interactive Hotspot to the red shape in the Nav2 track.

2. Make the target of the hotspot the **Lesson 2** marker.

3. Add a third and final Interactive Hotspot to the last shape in the Nav3 track.

4. Make the target of the hotspot the **Lesson 3** marker.

5. **PC users only:** On the Timeline, resize each of the Interactive Hotspot smaller so their playtime is no longer than the shapes. (If you allow the Interactive Hotspots to play longer than the images are onscreen, the video won't pause long enough for the learner to be able to click the shapes.)

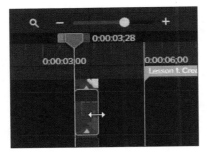

6. Share the project to **Screencast.com** with the Title **Working_with_Folders_Hotspots**.

7. Visit the lesson on Screencast.com and test any one of the hotspots. (If any of the hotspots cut off any audio, you can return to Camtasia and slide the markers a bit left or right on the Timeline and then republish to Screencast.com to test your changes.)

8. When finished, close the browser and then return to Camtasia.

9. Save your work. (Mac users, you can close the project.)

iCONLOGiC
"Skills and Drills" Learning

Module 8: Quizzes and Reporting Results

In This Module You Will Learn About:

- Quizzes, page 138
- Emailing Quiz Results, page 144
- Reporting Data to an LMS, page 148

And You Will Learn To:

- Add a Quiz and Multiple Choice Question, page 138
- Add a Fill In the Blank Question, page 141
- Use Screencast.com to Email Quiz Results, page 144
- Create a Content Package on the PC, page 148
- Create a Content Package on the Mac, page 151

Quizzes

I have never been a very good test-taker. The minute I hear a course I am taking includes a quiz, I fixate on the pending quiz or exam and get myself so stressed out that I stop learning.

It's only recently that I've come to understand quizzes and exams for what they are... an opportunity to learn. Had I thought of quizzes as just another part of the learning process, perhaps I wouldn't have stressed myself out so much and would have performed better on tests (there have been many poor performances over the years).

Many people compare eLearning to live training. It's not a fair comparison because eLearning lacks live, human interaction. In a live, instructor-led class, an experienced trainer can gauge the effectiveness of a lesson by asking the learner a question about something taught in the class. When a trainer asks questions, the learner has an opportunity to share what was learned, and prove lesson comprehension. It's perfectly fine for the learner in a live class to get a question wrong. In that instance, the trainer gives the correct answer and learning has taken place. In my classes, I typically ask direct and overhead questions of my students. If the answer given is wrong, I give the correct answer. Later, I'll ask that same learner the question again... only I reword the question (I'm sneaky like that). In almost every instance, the learner answers the rephrased question correctly.

Although an eLearning lesson cannot provide trainer-to-learner interaction, you can still engage the learner by adding a quiz to a Camtasia project. Each quiz can contain any or all of the following question types: Multiple choice, True/False, Fill in the blank, and Short answer.

> **Note:** If you intend to include a quiz in your eLearning lesson, you must produce the web version of your lesson (standalone videos cannot contain interactive elements such as a quiz).

Student Activity: Add a Quiz and Multiple Choice Question

1. Open **QuizMe** from the Camtasia2019Data Projects folder.

2. Position the Playhead where you'd like the quiz to appear.

   ☐ on the **Timeline**, position the **Playhead** just after the last Timeline object

3. Insert a quiz.

   ☐ from the list of tools at the left, click **Interactivity**

   ☐ click **Add Quiz to Timeline**

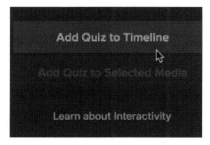

The quiz is created. Using the options on the Properties panel (in the upper right of the Camtasia window), you can name the quiz, add questions, preview the quiz, and more.

The quiz also appears on the Timeline with a default name, Quiz 1.

4. Rename the quiz.

    ☐ on the **Properties** panel, click **Quiz Options** (**Quiz Option Properties** on the Mac)

    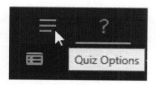

    ☐ change the Quiz Name to **Folders Quiz**

5. Ensure that the quiz will score.

    ☐ from just above the **Preview** button, ensure both **Viewers can see their results** and **Score Quiz** are selected

    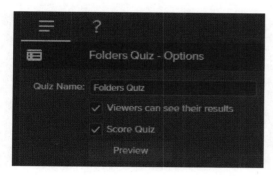

6. Specify the question type.

    ☐ on the Properties panel, click **Quiz Question Properties**

    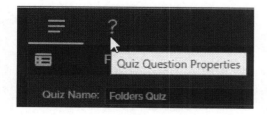

    ☐ from the **Type** drop-down menu, ensure **Multiple Choice** is selected

7. Edit the question.

   ☐ in the Question area, replace the placeholder text with **When giving a folder a name, how many characters can you use?**

8. Add four answers to the question.

   ☐ in the first Answer area, type **9**

   ☐ in the next Answer area, type **255**

   ☐ in the next Answer area, type **11**

   ☐ in the next Answer area, type **218**

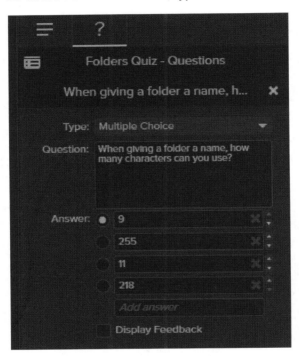

Note: You'll always end up with an extra "Add answer..." placeholder (as shown in the image above). No worries. Unless you type something in that placeholder, the answer will not be part of the quiz.

9. Specify a correct answer.

   ☐ click the circle next to the second answer, **255**

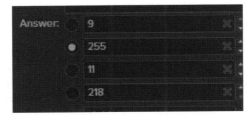

10. Save your work.

Student Activity: Add a Fill In the Blank Question

1. Ensure that the **QuizMe** project is open.

2. Add a question.

   ❏ from the bottom of the Properties panel, click **Add Question**

   The new question appears below the first.

   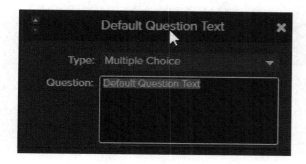

3. Specify the question type.

   ❏ from the **Type** drop-down menu, choose **Fill in the Blank**

4. Edit the question.

   ❏ replace the Question Text placeholder text with **The New Folder icon is found on the _____ tab of the Ribbon.**

5. Edit the Answer.

   ❏ in the **Answer** area, replace the placeholder text with **Home**

   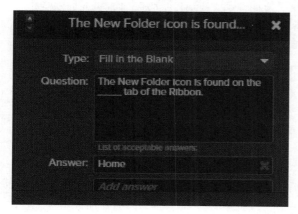

6. Save your work.

Quiz Confidence Check

1. Preview the quiz by clicking **See how Quiz looks in your viewer**.

A preview of the quiz appears on the Canvas.

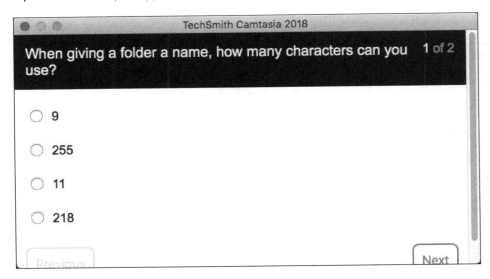

2. Select any of the answers in the first question and click the **Next** button (you'll likely need to scroll down to see the Next button).

3. Type anything you'd like into the text field within the **Fill in the Blank** question and then click the **Submit Answers** button.

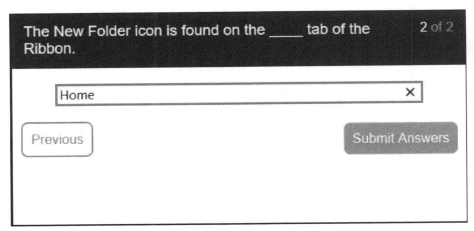

4. Click the **View Answers** button.

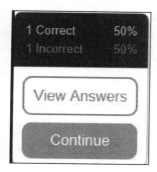

Correct answers are shown with a green check mark. Wrong answers are flagged with a red X.

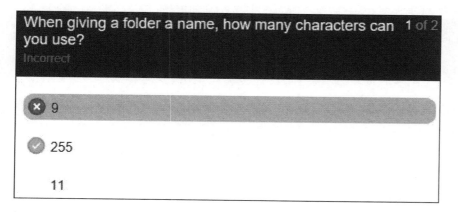

5. Close the Quiz preview.

6. Save the project. (Mac users, you can close the project.)

Emailing Quiz Results

When you Share your Camtasia project, you have seen that you can share it to YouTube and Vimeo. The problem with those to video-streaming services is that you can only upload videos. Any interactivity in your course is lost.

If you publish the finished project locally, the rendered files will only reside on your computer. Now what? How do your learners access to your content if it's only on your computer?

If you have a Learning Management System or web server of your own, you can upload the rendered output files there. But what if you don't have either of those? Where can you upload your content so that it is readily available and, if it contains interactivity such as hotspots or a quiz, ensure that the interactivity continues to work? Fortunately, TechSmith provides a free service called Screencast.com (you played with Screencast.com during the Confidence Check on page 131) where you can upload, test, and share your content with real learners. The project you are about to work with contains a quiz. You'll upload the lesson to Screencast.com and be able to test the quiz... and get quiz results from your learners via email.

> **Note:** You will need to create a free account on Screencast.com prior to starting the activity below. If you do not have an account, go to **www.screencast.com** and set one up now.

Student Activity: Use Screencast.com to Email Quiz Results

1. Open **ReportMe** from the Camtasia2019Data Projects folder.

2. Log-in to Screencast.com.

   ☐ choose **Share > Screencast.com**

   ☐ enter your Screencast.com email address and password

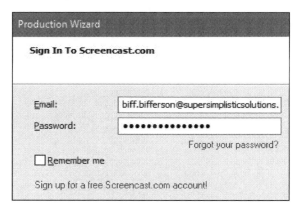

   ☐ **PC users**, click the **Next** button; **Mac users**, click the **Sign In** button

❏ leave the Video title as is

❏ **PC users**, click the **Next** button; **Mac users**, click the **Options** button

3. Set up the Quiz Reporting Options to send the quiz results to you via email.

    ❏ select **Report quiz results through email**

    ❏ in the Recipient email address and Confirm email address fields, type **your email address**

4. Require Viewer identity.

    ❏ from the **Viewer identity** area, select **Require viewers to input name & email address**

    ☑ Report quiz results through email

    Recipient email address: biff.bifferson@supersimplisticsolutions.com

    Confirm email address: biff.bifferson@supersimplisticsolutions.com

    - Quiz results are sent to this email address.
    - An incorrect email address cannot be changed.
    - Results are sent once per day if new data is present.

    Viewer identity
    ◯ Allow viewers to take quiz anonymously
    ⦿ Require viewers to input name & email address
        ☐ Allow viewers to skip the quizzes

    [Quiz appearance...]

❏ **PC users**, click the **Finish** button; **Mac users**, click **OK** button and then click the **Share** button

The lesson is produced and then automatically uploaded into your Screencast account.

Screencast Confidence Check

1. **PC users:** Switch to your web browser. You should already be logged into Screencast.com. If so, move to the next step. If you are not logged into Screencast.com, use a web browser to access Screencast.com and login. Once logged in, your uploaded video automatically opens.
Mac users: On the Share History window, click the Visit button.

2. Start the video and you will be prompted to identify yourself (thanks to the **Viewer identity** option you selected a moment ago).

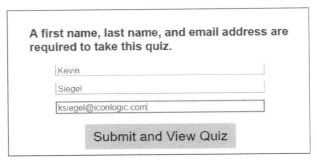

3. Fill in the fields with your first name, last name, and email address.

4. Click the **Submit and View Quiz** button.

5. When the time comes to take the quiz, take it. You can answer the questions correctly or incorrectly.

6. After taking the quiz, continue through to the end of the video. When finished, close the browser.

7. If you have access to email, check you email. The quiz results should be sent to you from Camtasia Quiz Service. The email comes from services@techsmith.com. If you don't see the email, you might want to check your SPAM folder and/or add TechSmith to your server's White List. (Also, it was several hours before I received my first email from TechSmith.)

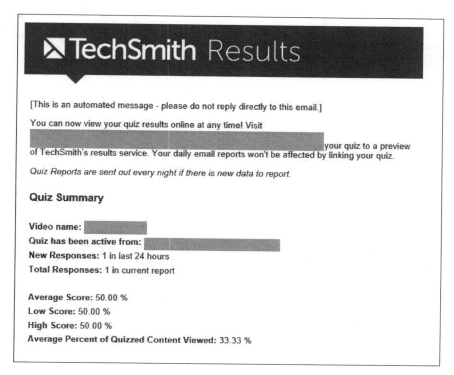

The Quiz results include a summary containing the number of responses, the average score, the low score, and the high score. Specific details about the quiz results are included as CSV files that can be opened with Microsoft Excel or other spreadsheet applications. The CSV files contain details about who took the quiz, the questions they got right and wrong, etc.

	A	B	C	D	E	F	G	H	I	J	K	L	M	N	O	P
	Display Na	Email Add	Quiz Nam	Question	Question	Question	Viewer Ar	Correct Ar	Answered	Percentag	Time to Co	Video Star	Quiz Finis	Video Nar	Video Duration	
	Kevin Sieg	ksiegel@i	Folders Qi	1	MC	When givi	9	255	No	33.33%		########	########	Screencas	0:03:12	
	Kevin Sieg	ksiegel@i	Folders Qi	2	FITB	The New I	Home	Home	Yes	33.33%		########	########	Screencas	0:03:12	

8. Close the e-mail (there is no need to save or send the e-mail).

9. Back in Camtasia, close any open dialog boxes and save your work.

Reporting Data to an LMS

Earlier in this module you uploaded content to Screencast.com and had the quiz result emailed to you. Many eLearning developers upload their training courses into a Learning Management System (LMS). At a minimum, an LMS handles issues related to providing learner access to the content, delivery of the content, and student performance tracking/reporting. In short, an LMS is the backbone of a web-based training system.

SCORM

Developed by public- and private-sector organizations, Sharable Content Object Reference Model (SCORM) is a series of eLearning standards that specify ways to catalog, launch, and track course objects. Courses and management systems that follow the SCORM specifications allow for sharing of courses among federal agencies, colleges, and universities. Although SCORM is not the only eLearning standard (AICC is another), SCORM is one of the most common. There are two primary versions of SCORM and they are both available in Camtasia—version 1.2, released in 1999, and version 2004.

Manifest Files

The Manifest file allows your published presentation to be used and launched from a SCORM 1.2- or 2004-compliant LMS. When you publish a project, you can have Camtasia create the Manifest file for you. The Manifest file that Camtasia creates contains XML tags that describe the organization and structure of the published project to the LMS.

During the activities that follow, you will create a content package (including a manifest file) suitable for upload into any SCORM-compliant LMS. (The steps are different enough between the PC and Mac that I've split them. PC users, you're up first below. Mac users, skip to page 151 for your steps to success.)

Student Activity: Create a Content Package on the PC

1. Ensure that the **ReportMe** project is still open.

2. Report quiz results using SCORM.

    ☐ choose **Share > Local File**

    ☐ choose **Custom Production Settings** from the drop down menu

    ☐ click **Next** a few times to advance to the **Quiz Reporting Options** screen

    ☐ deselect **Report quiz results through email**

    ☐ select **Report quiz results using SCORM**

    ☑ Report quiz results using SCORM
    ☐ Report quiz results through email

3. Set up the Manifest file.

    ☐ click the **SCORM Options** button

    The Manifest Options dialog box opens.

    ☐ change the **Course Title** to **Computer Basics**

☐ add the following **Description** text: **This course will teach you everything you ever wanted to know about computers but were afraid to ask.**

☐ change the **SCORM version** to **1.2**

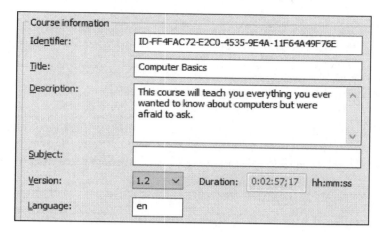

Some LMSs support SCORM version 1.2; some only support 2004, while others support both. Discuss the ideal version with your LMS vendor. (It's typically a safe bet to go with 1.2 if you are unsure.)

☐ change the **Lesson Title** to **Creating, Renaming, and Recycling Folders**

☐ from the **Quiz Success** area, set both values to **50%**

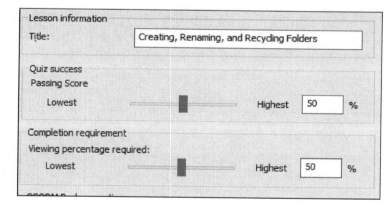

You only have two questions in your quiz so a 50% pass setting seems about right.

☐ from the **SCORM Package options** area, select **Produce zip file**

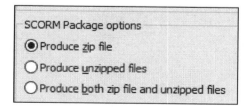

☐ click the **OK** button

☐ click the **Next** button

☐ change the Output file name to **ReportMeSCORM**

☐ ensure that the output folder is the **Camtasia2019Data > Produced_Videos**

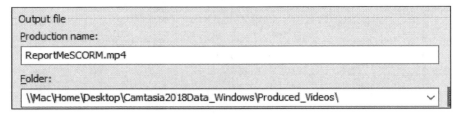

☐ click the **Finish** button

☐ once the rendering process is complete, click the **Open production folder** button

The zipped content package has been created, ready for you to upload into an LMS.

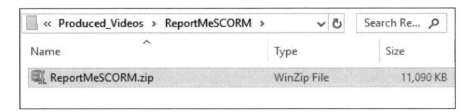

4. Close all windows.

5. Back in Camtasia, click the **Finish** button to close the Production results dialog box.

   The remaining steps in this module are for Mac users. You can move to the next module.

Student Activity: Create a Content Package on the Mac

1. Ensure that the **ReportMe** project is still open.

2. Report quiz results using SCORM.

   ☐ choose **Share > Local File**

   ☐ change the **Export As** file name to **ReportMeSCORM**

   ☐ ensure **Include Quiz** is selected and then click **Include SCORM**

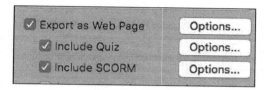

3. Set up the Manifest file.

   ☐ to the right of **Include SCORM**, click the **Options** button

   The Manifest Options dialog box opens.

   ☐ change the **Course Title** to **Computer Basics**

   ☐ add the following **Description** text: **This course will teach you everything you ever wanted to know about computers but were afraid to ask.**

   ☐ change the **SCORM version** to **1.2**

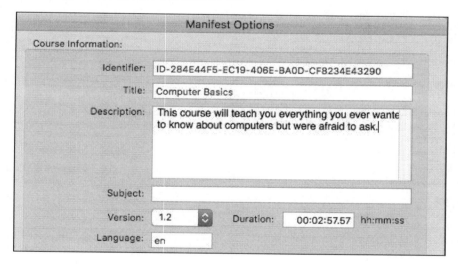

Some LMSs support SCORM version 1.2; some only support 2004, while others support both. Discuss the ideal version with your LMS vendor. (It's typically a safe bet to go with 1.2 if you are unsure.)

☐ change the **Lesson Title** to **Creating, Renaming, and Recycling Folders**

☐ from the **Quiz Success** area, set both values to **50%**

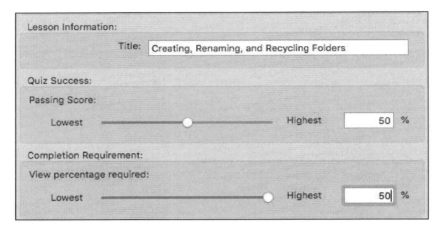

You only have two questions in your quiz so a 50% pass setting seems about right.

☐ from the **SCORM Package options** area, select **Produce zip file**

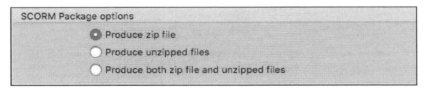

☐ click the **OK** button

☐ click the **Export** button

☐ once the Rendering process is complete, click the **Reveal in Finder** button

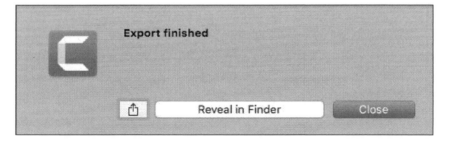

The zipped content package has been created, ready for you to upload into an LMS.

4. Close all windows.

5. Back in Camtasia, save and close the project.

iCONLOGiC

"Skills and Drills" Learning

Module 9: PowerPoint and Captions

In This Module You Will Learn About:

And You Will Learn To:

PowerPoint to Camtasia

I frequently meet eLearning developers who have created perfectly good Microsoft PowerPoint presentations and they'd like to use those presentations as eLearning. Unfortunately, PowerPoint does not have the ability to add quizzes, create SCORM packages, or automatically upload content to YouTube or Screencast.com. Rather than try to recreate the PowerPoint presentation from scratch in Camtasia, you have two ways to re-purpose existing PowerPoint content in Camtasia. PC users can record a PowerPoint presentation from within PowerPoint using a Camtasia Add-in. The finished recording will end up in a Camtasia project as a video on the Timeline. From there, you can add all of the awesome Camtasia-specific features to the project that you've learned about in this book. On the Mac side, there isn't a Camtasia Recorder Add-in for PowerPoint. However, you can get around this limitation by simply recording your presentation using Camtasia's screen recorder (you learned how to use the Recorder on page 48).

Another option is to bring some or all the PowerPoint slides into Camtasia as images.Those images, which will be imported into the Media Bin, can then be easily added to the Camtasia Timeline as needed.

You'll work with both options (recording using the PowerPoint recorder add-in) and importing PowerPoint as images) during the next few activities.

> **Note:** The next activity is for PC users only because the Camtasia add-in is not available on the Mac. **Mac users**, you can skip ahead to the activity on page 157.

Student Activity: Record PowerPoint on the PC

1. If Camtasia is running, close the program.

2. Open a PowerPoint presentation with Microsoft PowerPoint.

   ☐ using Microsoft PowerPoint, open **S3_Policies** from the **Camtasia2019Data > Other_Assets** folder

The Camtasia PowerPoint Add-in is automatically installed on your computer by the Camtasia application installer. Unless it has been disabled, you should be greeted with the alert dialog box below. (You can also confirm that the Camtasia Add-in has been installed by choosing **File > Options > Add-ins**.)

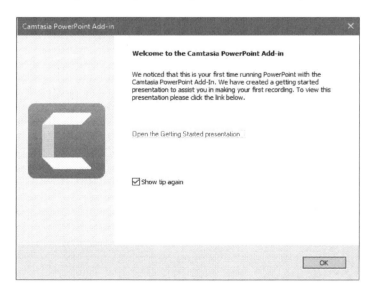

❏ click the **OK** button

❏ on the **Ribbon**, click the **Add-Ins** tab

Camtasia recording tools appear in the upper left of the PowerPoint window.

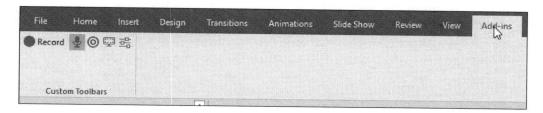

3. Record the PowerPoint presentation.

❏ from the **Custom Toolbars** area, click the **Record** tool

The PowerPoint slide show begins.

❏ in the lower right of the slide show, click the **Click to begin recording** button

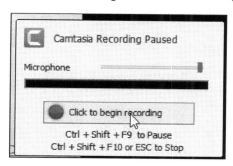

At this point, the presentation is being recorded, much like your screen was recorded when you learned to use Camtasia Recorder (on page 31).

❏ take your time and click in the middle of each slide to progress through the slide show

When you reach the end of the slide show, you'll be alerted with a dialog box.

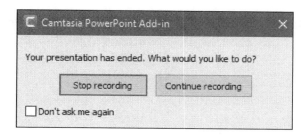

☐ click the **Stop Recording** button

Next you will be prompted to save the recording.

☐ navigate to **Camtasia2019Data** folder

☐ open the **Video_Files** folder and then save the file

You will be asked if you'd like to **Produce your recording** or **Edit your recording**. The former will take you directly to the Share options where you can elect to produce the video for Screencast.com, for YouTube, or as HTML5. The latter opens the recording in the Camtasia Editor where you can enhance the video using any of the production techniques you've learned to add during the lessons throughout this book (add annotations, audio, quizzes, behaviors, images, videos, etc.).

☐ select **Edit your recording**

☐ click the **OK** button

And that's that. Your PowerPoint presentation has been added to the Media Bin. At this point, you could move forward and produce and then Share the project as you have learned to do throughout this book.

Student Activity: Import PowerPoint Slides as Images

1. Create a new Camtasia project (there is no need to save previous projects).

2. Import PowerPoint slides into Camtasia as images, and then add an image to the Timeline.

   ☐ choose **File > Import > Media**

   ☐ from **Camtasia2019Data** > **Other_Assets**, open **S3_Policies**

   PC users, the PowerPoint slides are added to the Media Bin as individual images.
   Mac users, you'll see a window where you can elect to import all of the slides or select from a range of slides (you should import all of the slides).

Above, Mac users will see the option to import all of the PowerPoint slides or a range. (PC users will not see this option). At the right, the slides will end up in the Media Bin and can then be used on the Timeline as needed.

Note: If the import process does not work or you receive an error message, it might be helpful to start PowerPoint prior to attempting to import the slides into Camtasia and leave PowerPoint running. I've found that I receive errant "memory" error messages if PowerPoint isn't running on my system even though my computer has plenty of memory.

   ☐ on the **Media Bin**, right-click any image and choose **Add to Timeline at Playhead**

Before moving on, it might be useful to know that you can import a PowerPoint presentation into Camtasia by dragging and dropping. In the image below, notice that I'm dragging my PowerPoint file directly onto Camtasia's Media Bin (no need to click the Import Media button from within Camtasia).

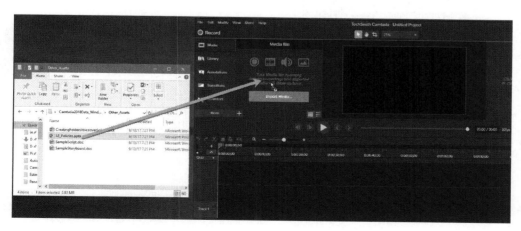

Closed Captions

Closed captioning allows you to provide descriptive information in your published eLearning project that typically matches the voiceover audio contained in your Camtasia project.

There are a couple of ways you can add closed captions to a Camtasia project. The following lessons show you how to add the captions manually (by transcribing), and how to create the Captions automatically via Speech-to-Text.

The process of creating closed captions is a bit different between the PC and Mac so I've split them up. PC users, your activity appears below. **Mac users**, you can skip ahead to the "Create Mac Closed Captions" module which begins on page 167.

Student Activity: Create PC Closed Captions

1. Open **CaptionMe** from the **Camtasia2019Data** Projects folder. (If prompted to save the project from the last activity, there is no need to do so.)

   There are seven audio clips in the Voiceover track. You're going to listen to the audio, painful if it might sound as if your typing skills aren't the best, and transcribe the audio you hear as closed captions.

2. Add captions manually.

   ☐ **PC users**, from the list of tools at the left, click **Captions** (if your display size is small, you might need to click the **More button** at the bottom of the list of tools and then click **CC Captions**)

   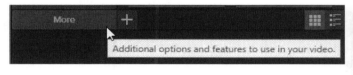

   ☐ on the **Timeline**, position the **Playhead** at exactly 5;00 (this is where the first voiceover audio clip is positioned)

   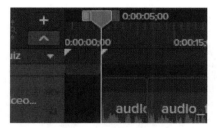

   ☐ on the **Canvas**, click the **Play** button and listen to the audio

   In this first audio segment, the narrator says: "Welcome to Super Simplistic Solutions learning series. This is lesson one: Creating New Folders."

   ☐ on the **Timeline**, re-position the **Playhead** at exactly 5;00

❏ click the **Add Caption** button

A Callout is added to both Track 4 and the Canvas.

❏ on the Canvas, type the following into the space beneath the background image: **Welcome to Super Simplistic Solutions learning series.**

3. Format the Caption text.

❏ click the **Font Properties** drop-down menu 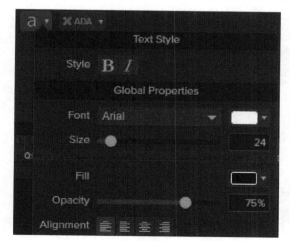 and change the **Size** to **24**

On the **Canvas**, the change to the font size is immediate. Keep in mind that the Captions aren't necessarily for your use—they're used by learners with a hearing disability. When creating eLearning content, you should avoid doing anything in your project that does not conform to the Americans with Disabilities Act (ADA).

NOTES

NOTES

In case you're not familiar with ADA, it's a 1990 US civil rights law that prohibits discrimination against individuals with disabilities in all areas of public life, including jobs, schools, transportation, and all public and private places that are open to the general public. Generally speaking, the law exists to ensure that people with disabilities have the same rights and opportunities as everyone else and guarantees equal opportunity for individuals with disabilities in public accommodations, employment, transportation, state and local government services, and even eLearning.

In the image below, notice that Camtasia obeyed your formatting instructions without complaint and made the font size smaller. However, the smaller font size is no longer ADA-compliant. How would you know that? Check out the **red X** and ADA text below the Caption, an indication that you are not compliant.

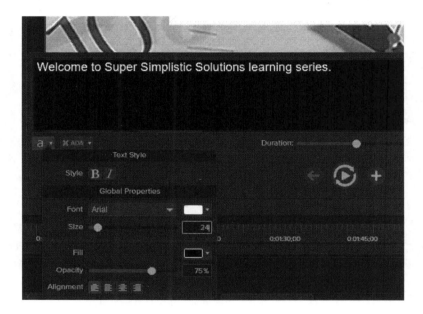

4. Ensure font formatting is ADA-compliant.

☐ click the **ADA Compliance** drop-down menu

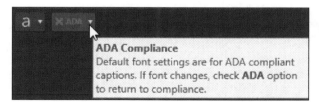

☐ choose **Make Compliant**

The font size and caption area are resized to conform to ADA standards.

5. Add another Caption.

   ☐ on the **Timeline**, position the Playhead to the right of the first Caption

   ☐ click the **Add Caption** button

   ☐ in the space below the Canvas, type **This is lesson one: Creating New Folders.**

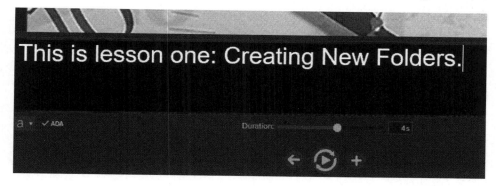

6. Preview the Captions.

   ☐ on the Timeline, deselect all objects

   ☐ position the **Playhead** as far **left** as it can go

   ☐ on the **Canvas**, click the **Play** button to preview the lesson

   With none of the Captions selected on the Timeline, you will get a fairly accurate preview of what learners see when they click the CC button on the Controller.

   Notice that the timing of the Captions does not exactly match the voiceover audio. You'll fix that next.

Student Activity: Control PC Caption Timing

1. Ensure that the **CaptionMe** project is open.

2. Adjust Caption Timing

   ☐ on the **Timeline**, drag the **right** edge of the **first** Caption to the left a bit to shorten its play time

   ☐ on the **Timeline**, drag the **right** edge of the **second** Caption to the left a bit to shorten its play time

   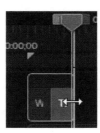

   ☐ on the Timeline, deselect all objects

   ☐ position the **Playhead** as far **left** as it can go

   ☐ on the **Canvas**, click the **Play** button to preview the lesson

   The Caption timing is a bit better but might still need work. You'll get a chance to tweak the timing a bit more and add another Caption during the Confidence Check that follows.

PC Captions Confidence Check

1. If the Caption timing needs it, spend a few moments making further adjustments.

2. Add a third Callout just to the right of the first two containing this text: **This lesson is going to teach you how to create a new folder on your computer.**

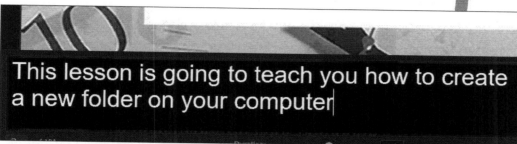

3. Preview the project from the beginning to see your new Caption.

4. If necessary, make adjustments to the Caption's timing so it matches the audio as closely as possible.

5. Share the project as a Local File. (Select Custom Production Settings.)

6. Click the **Next** button twice.

7. When you get to the Smart Player Options, click the **Options** tab.

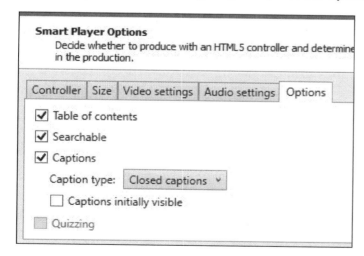

From this screen, you can enable or disable Captions and make their default state "visible" or "on by default." The standard practice is to make Captions not visible by default, so this option is fine as is.

8. Click the remaining **Next** buttons and the Finish button to finish the rendering process.

9. In the browser, click the **CC** button to view the Captions you added.

10. Close the browser window.

11. Back in Camtasia, close the Production Results window.

    Now you'll get a chance to copy and paste text from an existing voiceover script.

12. Minimize Camtasia and, from the **Camtasia2019Data**, **Other_Assets** folder, open **CreatingFoldersVoiceoverScript**.

> **Audio File 1:**
> Welcome to Super Simplistic Solutions learning series.
> This is lesson one: Creating New Folders.
>
> **Audio File 2:**
> This lesson is going to teach you how to create a new folder on your computer, how to rename it, and how to both delete and restore recycled items.
>
> **Audio File 3:**
> When creating folders keep in mind that you can create as many folders as you need.

13. In the **Audio File 2** text, select **"how to rename it, and how to both delete and restore recycled items"** and copy the text to the Clipboard.

14. Return to Camtasia and the CaptionMe project.

15. Position the Playhead just to the right of your existing Captions.

16. Create a new Caption and paste the text you copied into the space beneath the Canvas.

17. Save your work.

Student Activity: Use Speech-to-Text to Create PC Closed Captions

1. Ensure that the **CaptionMe** project is open.

2. Delete the existing Captions.

   ☐ on the **Timeline**, right-click the Captions on **Track 4** and choose **Delete**

3. Create Captions using Speech-to-Text.

   ☐ from the list of tools at the left, click **Captions**

   ☐ from the upper left of the Captions panel, click **Script Options** (the **gear** icon)

   ☐ choose **Speech-to-Text**

You'll receive some tips for improving the Speech-to-Text feature. Later, after you've had a chance to work with Camtasia, you should try some of these tips and see how they might improve your Speech-to-Text results. For this activity, you're going to use the default settings to see where they take you.

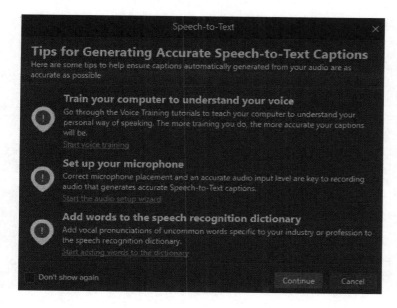

   ☐ click the **Continue** button

Camtasia listens to the voiceover audio in the background and, like magic, creates Captions on Track 4.

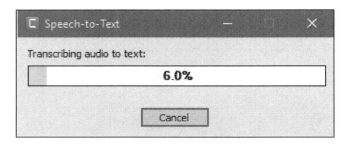

When you move through the Timeline, you'll see that not all of the Captions are ready to Share (you'd have to go through them and spend some time editing). However, most people who use this feature agree that it's faster to go this route than transcribe the audio from scratch.

> this lesson is going to teach you how to create a new folder a new computer Halloween name it and how both the leap and restore recycled

You've learned three ways to add Captions: transcribing, copy/paste, and Speech-to-Text. I've had the best luck using the copy/paste technique (that assumes you have a voiceover script that has already been created). I've also found that Speech-to-Text, given enough customization/tweaking, yields higher than average returns.

4. Save your project.

5. Exit Camtasia.

The remaining activities in this book are for Mac users.

Congratulations, you have completed my book. I'm hoping you are now comfortable creating Camtasia projects from scratch, recording screen actions, and adding such Camtasia media and assets as videos, callouts, images, behaviors, audio, quizzes, and captions. You should also feel comfortable in your ability to Share your content locally, on YouTube, and on Screencast.com.

Should you get stuck using Camtasia, the first place to look for help is online via the TechSmith Camtasia website (http://techsmith.com) and TechSmith blog (blogs.techsmith.com/category/tips-how-tos/). TechSmith has a great community offering free tips, tricks, and step-by-step videos covering all things Camtasia. You can also email me should you need a nudge in the right direction at **ksiegel@iconlogic.com**.

Student Activity: Create Mac Closed Captions

1. Save and close any open projects.

2. Open **CaptionMe** from the **Camtasia2019Data** Projects folder.

   There are several audio clips in the Voiceover track. You're going to listen to some of the clips and manually create a few Captions.

3. Add captions manually.

   ☐ from the **Tools** panel at the left, click **Audio Effects**

   ☐ from the list of Audio Effects, drag **Captions** on top of the first audio clip in the Voiceover Track (on the Timeline)

   The Caption Track opens just above the Timeline.

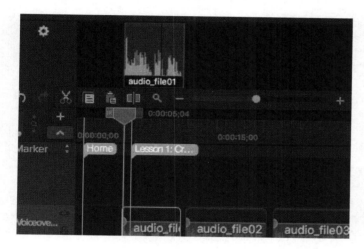

   ☐ on the **Caption Track**, click the **left side** of the audio waveform

   The first part of the audio plays and a typing area opens. In this first audio segment, the narrator says: **Welcome to Super Simplistic Solutions learning series. This is lesson one: Creating New Folders.**

   ☐ type the following into the space beneath the background image: **Welcome to Super Simplistic Solutions learning series.**

The Caption you typed automatically appears on the Canvas. This is what a learner will see if they decide to use the lesson's closed captions.

4. Format the Caption text.

☐ on the **Caption Track**, click the left side of the audio waveform again

☐ click the **Change font properties for captions** tool

Font options appear at the top of the Canvas.

☐ change the font size to **18**

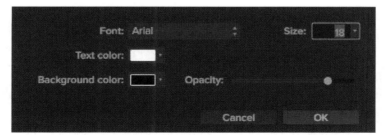

☐ click the **OK** button

On the Canvas, the change to the font size is immediate. And you are likely thinking to yourself that the smaller font size looks better than the clunky, larger font. However, keep in mind that the Captions aren't necessarily for you—they're for learners who cannot hear the audio. When creating eLearning content, you'll need to be on the alert to anything you might do in your project that does not conform to the Americans with Disabilities Act (ADA).

In case you're not familiar with ADA, it's a 1990 US civil rights law that prohibits discrimination against individuals with disabilities in all areas of public life, including jobs, schools, transportation, and all public and private places that are open to the general public. Generally speaking, the law exists to ensure that people with disabilities have the same rights and opportunities as everyone else and guarantees equal opportunity for individuals with disabilities in public accommodations, employment, transportation, state and local government services, and even eLearning.

In the case of font sizes used in Captions, a larger font is preferred because it is simply easier to see.

5. Restore the Caption's font size to its larger size.

   ❑ on the **Caption Track**, click the left side of the audio waveform again

   ❑ click the **Change font properties for captions** tool

   ❑ change the font size back to **32**

   ❑ click the **OK** button

6. Add another Caption.

   ❑ on the **Caption Track**, click the **right** side of the audio waveform

   ❑ type **This is lesson one: Creating New Folders.**

7. Preview the Captions.

☐ position the **Playhead** as far **left** as it can go

☐ on the **Canvas**, click the **Play** button to preview the lesson

Notice that the timing of the captions does not exactly match the voiceover audio (the first Caption is onscreen a bit too long). You'll fix that next.

Student Activity: Control Mac Caption Timing

1. Ensure that the **CaptionMe.cmproj** project is open.

2. Adjust Caption Timing

   ☐ on the **Caption Track**, click the **left side** of the audio waveform

   ☐ from the bottom right of the caption screen, change the **Duration** to **3** seconds

   ☐ on the Timeline, position the **Playhead** as far **left** as it can go

   ☐ on the **Canvas**, click the **Play** button to preview the lesson

   The Caption timing is more in sync with the voiceover audio.

Mac Captions Confidence Check

1. Add a caption to the second audio file on the Timeline with the following text: **This lesson is going to teach you how to create a new folder on your computer,**

2. Share the project to Screencast.com. (Prior to clicking the Share button, choose **Closed captions** from the **Caption style** area.)

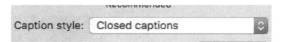

3. After the Export process is complete, Visit the page.

4. After starting the lesson, click the **CC** button on the playbar to view the Captions you added.

5. Close the browser window.

   Now you'll get a chance to copy and paste text from an existing voiceover script.

6. Hide Camtasia (to get it out of your way for a moment) and, from the **Camtasia2019Data > Other_Assets** folder, open **CreatingFoldersVoiceoverScript**.

   Audio File 1:
   Welcome to Super Simplistic Solutions learning series.
   This is lesson one: Creating New Folders.

   Audio File 2:
   This lesson is going to teach you how to create a new folder on your computer, how to rename it, and how to both delete and restore recycled items.

   Audio File 3:
   When creating folders keep in mind that you can create as many folders as you need.

7. In the **Audio File 2** text, select **"how to rename it, and how to both delete and restore recycled items"** and copy the text to the Clipboard.

8. Return to Camtasia and the CaptionMe project.

9. Still working in the section caption, click the right side of the waveform and paste the text you copied into the caption text area.

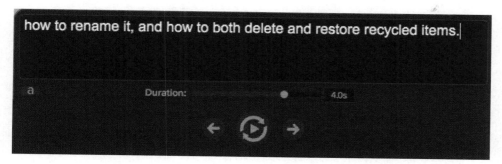

10. Save your work.

11. Close the project.

Congratulations, you have completed my book. I'm hoping you are now comfortable creating Camtasia projects from scratch, recording screen actions, and adding such Camtasia media and assets as videos, callouts, images, behaviors, audio, quizzes, and captions. You should also feel comfortable in your ability to Share your content locally, on YouTube, and on Screencast.com.

Should you get stuck using Camtasia, the first place to look for help is online via the TechSmith Camtasia website (http://techsmith.com) and TechSmith blog (blogs.techsmith.com/category/tips-how-tos/). TechSmith has a great community offering free tips, tricks, and step-by-step videos covering all things Camtasia. You can also email me should you need a nudge in the right direction at **ksiegel@iconlogic.com**.

Notes

Index

NOTES

Notes

Made in the USA
Middletown, DE
14 January 2020